English Grammar Rules 101

10 Essential Rules to Improve Your Writing, Speaking and Literature Skills for Students and Beginners

MELONY JACOBS

TABLE OF CONTENTS

1 **Introduction**   Pg #8

2 **Background – The Origins of The English Language**   Pg #14

3 **Rule 1 – Master The Basics**   Pg #29

4 **Rule 2 – Familiarize With Key Grammar Components**   Pg #54

5 **Rule 3 – The 4 H's: Homonyms, Homophones, Homographs and Heteronyms**   Pg #66

6 **Rule 4 – Become a Punctuation Pro**   Pg #77

7 **Rule 5 – Perfect Past, Present and Future Tense**   Pg #113

8 **Rule 6 – Structuring Sentences With Ease**   Pg #132

9 **Rule 7 – Conquer Capitalization**   Pg #145

10 **Rule 8 – Spell Correctly and Format Efficiently** Pg #153

11 **Rule 9 – Create Killer Compositions** Pg #163

12 **Rule 10 – Add Your Personal Touch** Pg #168

13 **Bonus Rule – Never Neglect Common Grammar Mistakes** Pg #174

14 **Conclusion** Pg #181

INTRODUCTION

Writing is something many of us do on a daily basis. Yet few of us feel truly confident to say we are a great writer. When you read something that is written well, it can be very powerful. Good writing can inspire people to get up and act, make them feel incredibly moved, or make them really mad. This is because the best writing transports you to a place where you see and feel what you are reading as if it were really happening to you.

It is fair to say that we can all recognize the difference between good and bad writing and that we can acknowledge how important it is to write well. However, when office employees were asked whether they prioritized improving their writing skills over other professional skills, the answer was almost always no.

We all learned how to read and write in school. For most of us, that is where our writing education ended. The main problem with this is that the quality of education on English grammar varies so much depending on when and where you went to school. Not to mention, for a long time, English language education adopted an intuitive approach that saw students gaining grammatical knowledge through reading rather than rote learning. This method of learning has a lot to be responsible for when it comes to a whole generation not being able to tell the difference between there and their.

The result of not knowing your way around English grammar can often turn into a source of embarrassment for many of us. It might even have led to you being publicly outed by a coworker for your repeated misuse of you're. What is worse, because we have been making the same grammatical mistakes for years, it is almost impossible to spot on your own that you are making them. I am certain that what led you to pick up this book was some incident or other that involved being shamed for making an obvious grammatical mistake. Don't fear, we are all grammatical offenders here and what matters most is that you have recognized the need to do something about it!

In all truthfulness, nearly all of us make repeated grammatical mistakes and we all need to take the time to polish up on our writing skills. The impact of taking a really small amount of time out of your day to improve your English grammar knowledge will be massive. In no time at all, you can use the super simple tips in this book to power up your writing and impress your boss with the strength of your well-written proposals or whatever it is you need to write.

This book is supercharged with all the essential knowledge you need to know to improve your use of English grammar. How long will it take you to get through this book? It will take you a little more than a month to read and practice the tips and techniques presented in this book. You will quickly progress from zero to grammatical hero by simply following this book step by step.

As a way of a quick intro on me, I am Melody Jacobs, a 52 year old avid book reader and expert grammar corrector. As a professional editor and proofreader, it is my job to fix people's grammatical mistakes. So in truth, I don't want the whole country to all of a sudden become grammatical experts, or I would be out of a job! What my experience has taught me is most errors that people make in their writing are about grammar and that they repeat these errors over and over, most likely as they don't realize they are making them. It isn't just in the texts I am proofing that I see errors, they also appear in the many published novels that I consume weekly. The reality is we are a nation of grammar offenders and mistakes are so common we are starting to think they are correct.

So, with this, I decided that rather than quietly complaining to my husband and friends about the raft of grammatical mistakes I see on a daily basis, I thought I would take my knowledge of the most common errors and set out to write this book. The main aim of the book is to provide an incredibly practical and quick way to improve your English grammar. You can take advantage of my extensive experience with understanding why people make mistakes. You can save yourself a lot of time and pain by spending this short time learning about grammar. After that, you can rest assured that what you learn in this book will massively impact your writing almost immediately.

In the end, grammar is something that is right or wrong. There is no gray area. This is something which you can be happy about as once you have it down, you are good. However, I am fairly certain that you will have probably picked up this book because your grammar is holding you back and you have decided it is time to fix it. Poor grammar really does stand in your way of achieving the highest grades at school, being thought of as an outstanding employee, and ultimately being able to express yourself correctly whenever you speak or write.

That is why I give you my word that with this simple and quick to read guide on English grammar rules, you will be fully equipped to manage any grammatical situation. I promise you that you won't feel like a floundering fish when you are put on the spot to produce a grammatically correct sentence structure. Instead, the grammar rules will be instilled within you so that you can respond with confidence and ease. On your end, a level of commitment is needed in order to practice what is outlined within this book. If you only read through this book once and do not practice the grammar rules, you will soon forget them and return to your bad habits. It is essential that you dedicate yourself to making a lasting change within this area. You only need to input a very small amount of effort to see a massive return. It is like riding a bike, once learned, it is not easily forgotten.

With this guide in hand and by using the personalized techniques described within, you will be on the road to English grammar perfection faster than you could ever have imagined. My previous students have all raved about how quickly they mastered the techniques and how stepping up their English grammar game has massively helped them in all areas of life. Now, I hope that with this book I can combine all of my knowledge on the most effective way to teach grammar and encourage a much larger amount of people to improve their grammar then I am able to with just my one to one lessons.

So, come on! Jump in and start practicing. Tomorrow you will already be better than today with your use of English grammar. Good things are waiting for you, just as soon as you can express yourself effectively and are able to show the world that you are an English grammar aficionado.

BACKGROUND – THE ORIGINS OF THE ENGLISH LANGUAGE

There is no denying the importance of English as a language, with over 2 billion speakers worldwide. English is the lingua franca of the world, meaning it is the language used for communication between speakers of other languages. Its dominance as a language came to force largely in the last few centuries because it was the language spoken in the British Empire who spread the language to over ⅓ of the world's population including the USA, Canada, and Australia. The cultural production that then came out of the USA in the 20th century, and continues to this day, saw a worldwide audience consume English language media in the form of popular music and blockbuster movies. Particularly amongst the younger generations across the world, you are very likely to find that even if they don't speak English, they are aware of it and can understand some of it. English is significant enough that the majority of countries across the world use it as a second language on signs, menus in restaurants and anything that might be read by a non-native language speaker for that area. Given the continued prominence of USA made music, movies, and tv shows, it doesn't seem that English will be giving up its place of prominence anytime soon.

English is a Western Germanic language that was first spoken around the 5th CE when settlers from the areas around Germany, Denmark, and the Netherlands first came to the British Isles. These people were known as the Anglo-Saxons, hence where the Anglo bit of English comes from. The Anglo-Saxons were called Anglo because they came from an area of land that looked a bit like a fish hook. The Proto-Indo-European root of a fish hook came from the world angle, meaning it was bent. The modern English word angling, meaning fishing, also comes from this root. One theory is that the word Anglo is meant to mean fishermen and that English is the language of the fishermen, a theory that fits with both the fact that the Anglo-Saxons came from an area of low lying sea and that the British Isles were mainly full of fishermen and their families.

Previous to speaking English, the people of the British Isles spoke different native Celtic language dialects that were mainly influenced by Norse, a Nordic language brought to the area by Vikings in the centuries before this. Some influences of these Viking invaders still linger on in the English language, such as Thursday whose original meaning is Thor's day, the day to celebrate the Viking god Thor. In the United Kingdom today, the people in Wales, Scotland and Ireland still speak the Celtic languages which are distinctly different from English.

The first form of English was Old English. To a speaker of Modern English, this version is almost unintelligible. For example, the famous Beowulf poem written in Old English starts off with the following, "Hƿæt! ƿē Gār-Dena in ġeār-dagum, þēod-cyninga, þrym ġefrūnon, hū ðā æþelingas ellen fremedon," which in Modern English translates to "Lo! We have heard of the majesty of the Spear-Danes, of those nation-kings in the days of yore, and how those noblemen promoted zeal." As is clear to see, it is no small feat to read and understand Old English. The alphabet is extended to include extra letters and the words themselves are much closer to Modern German than Modern English. The grammar is also much closer to Modern German, something which is important to understand later when trying to get your head around Modern English grammar. The truth is, Modern German grammar is considerably more logical than English.

If we had stuck with the grammar system we inherited with Old English, then I am certain that our modern grammar would be much easier to understand. However, as you will see next, the evolution of the English language jumped into the much more complicated and exception filled pool of the French language. Blame William the Conqueror.

1066, the Battle of Hastings sees the English King Harold killed by an arrow shot through his eye and William the Conqueror from Normandy, France, takes over the English throne. Over the next 100 years, a distinct shift can be seen on the British Isles with an old version of French becoming the language of the court and Old English being relegated to the language of the poor. Slowly but surely, a combined language starts to emerge, known as Middle English, which was still distinctly Western Germanic but which was now undeniably influenced by Franco grammar and Latin vocabulary. This form of English does have some resemblance to Modern English and when read it is a little bit intelligible. For example, the first line of the Canterbury Tales by Geoffery Chaucer reads in the original language as, "Whan that Aprill, with his shoures soote. The dro3te of March hath perced to the roote. And bathed every veyne in swich licour, Of which vertu engendred is the flour;" which transcribes as, "When [that]

April with his showers sweet. The drought of March has pierced to the root. And bathed every vein in such liquor, Of which virtue engendered is the flower;" Now we begin to see the emergence of Modern English as it is not such a great leap from Middle English to what we speak now.

Starting from the 15th century, English started to really take form. Three major things happened in the 17th century that have had a lasting impact on the language until today. The first event was the Bible being translated from Latin to English for the first time. This meant that common people who were able to read had greater access to the religion than before and could read the Bible even if they didn't speak Latin. The King James Bible is considered to be one of the earliest texts written in Modern English and as it was such an important text it found its way into many homes across England, leading to a standardization of the language that had not been seen before.

Next came William Shakespeare. As a playwright, Shakespeare is responsible for shaping the way we speak English today. He invented hundreds of words that we still use, such as critic, lonely, and swagger. What is more, he also heavily influenced the use of grammar and sentence structure. Previous to the emergence of Modern English, which Shakespeare is attributed to as writing in, the language was not standardized and the use of phrases was very rare. Due to the love of Shakespeare's plays throughout England, the phrases he invented became commonplace, such as 'with bated breath' and 'a foregone conclusion'. Not only were his phrases commonly used but the idea of phrases became the norm with more and more invented by writers and poets being used by the common people.

The last event that took place during this period is the Great Vowel Shift. This is an event that changed forever the way that we pronounce English words, specifically the way we pronounce vowels. Before the shift, lots of English words had long vowel sounds and the spelling of them reflected this. However, after the shift, the vowel sounds were shortened and the use of silent consonants became common, such as in the word thumb where you do not pronounce the b. From this time onwards, approximately the middle to late 17th century, English spelling was standardized further and these standardizations are still in place today.

Does that mean that the English language has not changed

since William Shakespeare? No, of course, it has changed. Every language evolves over time, as can be seen by the different stages of the language that have just been described. What is important to know is that even though we may not speak like Shakespeare, for example in his play A Midsummer Night's Dream his character Lysander declares, "Ay me! for aught that I could ever read, Could ever hear by tale or history, The course of true love never did run smooth;" it is still intelligible, the vocabulary is still used today, and the grammar structure is correct.

Since William Shakespeare, English has gone on a real journey of discovery which has twisted its fate towards a number of different paths. English has traveled the world, been part of the history of the empire and is now spoken by millions of people as a first language and even more as a second language. The English spoken today is still considered Modern English but it has morphed into different dialects, for example, British English is a distinct dialect, as is American English. A dialect is different than a language. When you speak a different language to another person, you should expect that you will not understand most of it. You may understand some of the vocabulary, for example, if the language comes from the same family of languages such as French and Spanish. With a dialect, you should expect to understand most of the vocabulary, but the grammar can be different and there will certainly be a lot of regional vocabulary that will differ, usually the names of items. So, a British person can easily understand an American, but they definitely had some humorous moments discovering the different meanings they have for common words. Such as, a rubber is an eraser to a British person, where it is a condom to an American!

More important than the difference between dialects, is the way that English is now written. Until around 150 years ago, the majority of people who spoke English could not read or write it. What this meant is that there existed a huge variance in the way that people from different areas would speak English. If you were living in Northern England, you would certainly use a lot of words and phrases that would be foreign to someone living in London. The same goes if you talk about someone living in Toronto 100 years ago, they would not be able to fully understand what someone was saying in Vancouver. Regional variances were very common in the spoken language. However, as the only people to read and write were of the educated classes and represented a small percentage of the English speaking population, the variance amongst the written language was restricted. More than that, large amounts of control were placed upon the way people wrote English. Grammar was thought of as something that must be used correctly and if you did not you would be strictly reprimanded. To write anything in informal English was considered very bad practice and therefore the written form of English did not see much alteration for hundreds of years after Shakespeare, that was until the contemporary period we are in now.

The big shift came when education was opened up to the masses. In the 20th century, being able to read and write was no longer a privilege of the upper classes. As free education for children was provided in many English speaking countries, this also meant a much larger percentage of the population being able to read and write. This was an education revolution and English speaking countries became the first to reach almost complete literacy in their population. As much as this was incredibly important for opening up education for all, the formalization of the English language did take a bit of a hit. Now a much larger number of people could read and write and this meant that there was no way to control how English was written in any way the same way it was before. During the first waves of literacy, regional words were the first to be introduced to written English. Phrases and words from the different parts of the English speaking world were written down for the very first time. People were slow to standardize the spelling and grammatical use of these phrases and so until the Oxford Dictionary was able to categorize them correctly, the written language became a bit of a mess. In particular, people started to use grammar very informally and in large parts, wrongly. For example, a very common phrase that came out of North West England was, "I didn't do nothing wrong." In this phrase, the grammar is incorrect as you can't have a double negative. Didn't is negative and nothing is negative. Essentially, they should cancel each other out and should be understood as 'I did something." However, as this phrase was known widely in this area and they accepted it to mean, "I didn't do anything wrong," it was written down by a lot of people from this area. Does that mean that the grammar changed because of these new additions? No, the grammar rules still remain the same and this is not considered strictly correct. What it did do is bring about the difference between formal written English and informal written English.

As we entered the last decade of the 20th century, we saw a massive acceleration of the informalization of written English. Firstly, slang became more widely used in written English. Slang has always been around whenever English has been spoken. People like to make up their own words, they like to associate words with their hobbies, people they are friends with, or perhaps a subculture they are part of. What happened in the 1990s is that these subcultures started to go mainstream, with the music, movies and tv-shows that were produced about them being accessible to large parts of the English speaking population. Hip-hop is a strong example of a subculture from the USA that through the power of media, affected the way an English speaking person in Manchester, England spoke. Young people started to say phrases such as, "you are da bomb," and "why you got beef?" After a while, the more that young people say these phrases, the more they start to write them down. This understandably, affects the way that grammar is understood and used as neither of the above examples are grammatically correct, but people start to think they are correct as they become common and this, in turn, challenges how they think of grammar. Unfortunately, the result is usually negative as they start to apply grammar rules incorrectly and make grammar mistakes such as saying, "why you here?" rather than, "why are you here?"

Secondly, came the cell phone with the ability to send SMS messages to your friends and family. As some of you may remember, the qwerty keyboard did not exist on the first phones. Instead, you texted by pressing the numbers 1-9 for different letters. The process could be quite long, so the result was people throwing grammar rules out of the window and inventing shorthand ways to say sentences. For example, "I am going to be late tonight," was transcribed to text speak as, "I'm gonna be L8 tonite." This style of written English became commonplace for users of cell phones and they continued to shorten phrases to the bare minimum, such as LOL standing for laughing out loud and BRB meaning be right back. The impact of this was massive upon the way that the younger generations started to use written English. Teachers throughout the English speaking world come to massively resent the coming of cell phones, as they now spent large amounts of time correcting their students written and spoken English.

Finally, the internet came and established the use of informal written English as the norm. By the beginning of the 21st century, a large majority now had access to the internet and were able to communicate with people across the world in English. With the advent of social media, sending quick messages to your friends was very normal, as was posting a status about what you were doing. Trends in language use would vary over the next ten years with different words being fashionable at different times, such as swag, binge-watch, and woke. These words aren't really massively significant as, throughout the history of language, they have always adapted and added in new vocabulary. What is significant, is the confirmation that informal written English was here to stay.

The importance of seeing how the written form of English has transformed over the last century is that it has made us all really bad at grammar. On a daily basis, we consume large amounts of written language that is predominantly written in informal English with grammar rules being loosely applied. People continue to use text speak regularly, with speed being seen as a quality more desirable over the accuracy of grammar. Yes, it is true that a lot of people who you are around on a daily basis probably understand how you speak and how you write, even if you use informal language. However, a person in Australia may not understand an American when they write online that they, "are totally shook by finding out the tea." Nor would that American understand when the Australian said, "whack a snag on the barbie."

The consequences, therefore, of informal language being so commonplace and how it has transferred into the written form, is that we have lost clarity across the English language. It is completely fine to speak and write in different ways depending on who you are talking to. You can use informal language with your friends and family as it feels natural and comfortable. But, when you use this same language with people you don't know, who may not be from the same area, or even the same country as you, you risk them not understanding. That is why formal English exists, it allows all speakers of English to understand each other, independent of where they come from. What is more, as the grammar rules are standardized, it also allows you to be certain that what you are saying will be understood and not misinterpreted. So when you say, "I am very shocked by what I heard about Sally," rather than "I am totally shook by finding out the tea," nothing will be misunderstood.

Don't underestimate how important being understood is. As you have seen throughout this chapter, the English language has taken many forms and has shifted over time into what it is today. However, nothing has prepared us for the assault upon the formal language that is happening now. So, when you do make the effort to learn how to apply grammar correctly and write in formal English when at school and at work, you will be marked out quickly as above your peers for the quality of your written work. It is still a very much admired quality in an employee and further than that, if you do want to progress to the higher levels of your chosen career, it is considered unacceptable to use anything other than formal English. What is more, when you use formal English and correct grammar, you can be assured that your million-dollar ideas are understood clearly, and may even make you that million dollars! Take this time to focus on your grammar, think of it as an investment for your future and a stepping stone to where it is you want to be in life.

RULE 1 – MASTER THE BASICS

First things first, whenever you write anything, you use the building blocks of the English language. Without them, we wouldn't have a language, just a collection of words that people would say.

The funny thing is though, most of us can't identify a verb from a noun or an adjective from an adverb. And the truth is, this really isn't your fault. Yes, you may have seen them written up on a board somewhere back in your school days, but rarely would any teacher have spent much longer than an afternoon teaching you exactly the meaning of each different building block.

That is because, when you are teaching a first language, you don't start from the beginning and ensure that your students really know what each part is. Instead, you skip ahead to reading longer texts to develop their level of the language quickly. However, as a student, when you miss these building blocks and don't understand them fully, you can carry that misunderstanding through to adulthood and repeatedly make the same grammar mistakes.

So when you are in a tangle over your adverbs and adjectives, stop blaming yourself. Rather, you must recognize that now is the time to detangle the mess and to build up correctly the way you write and speak.

The doing block: understanding verbs

Without a verb, you don't have a language, just a collection of words that can't be understood. That is because a verb is any word that describes what someone or something is doing. You can also think of it as an action word to help you remember that a verb is always about performing an action.

I **run** every day by the lake.

In this example, **run** is the verb because it clearly expresses that the person is performing an action, in this case, that action is running.

I **love** Jessica because she is funny and sweet.

In this example, **love** is the verb because it shows what someone is doing. Don't get confused that verbs can only be a visible action such as walking or talking. That is why it is much better to think of them as a doing word. To love someone is to do something. That is how we can clearly identify that this word is a verb.

Pretty much every time we speak or write, we need to express that we are doing something. That is why verbs are so important. If we try now to write a sentence without a verb, it doesn't turn out very well!

I to the cinema with friends.

Perhaps, you might be able to guess the meaning of this sentence, but it is obvious to everyone that it doesn't actually make sense. Being clear with your use of language is the ultimate goal. That is why, no matter what you write or speak about, you must include a verb.

It can be a little bit tricky to figure out what is a verb and what is not. That is why I want you to always remember it as something that you or someone else is doing. Keep this in mind, particularly when you look to the next description of a certain type of verbs called helper verbs.

Helping verbs are, as the name goes, incredibly helpful! They appear in many of the sentences that we write, so it is essential to identify them correctly as verbs.

I **will play** football later.

In this sentence, the action verb is **play.** It is easy to identify it as a verb as someone is doing something, which in this case is to play football. On top of this, there is another verb in this sentence and that is **will.** This is a helping verb as it is helping you understand the correct meaning of the other verb in the sentence.

If we remove the helping verb and the **later** at the end of the sentence, it now reads:

I **play** football.

This sentence has a different meaning to the previous sentence. As you can see, a helping verb can dramatically change the meaning of the sentence, so using them correctly is a must. What you have to remember is that a helping verb is usually not an obvious action, which is why people often dismiss them as not being a verb. Yet, if we look at other examples of helping verbs, you can see that they are about someone doing something.

I **am** Jessica.

In this example, the only verb in the sentence is a helping verb. This person is saying that they are Jessica. In being Jessica, they are doing something. What is more, in this example, the helping verb isn't actually helping anything. That is because not all helping verbs have to be written next to another verb for them to make sense.

What is important for you to remember is that 99% of the time, your sentence must include a verb. It can be a verb by itself, a verb with a helping verb, or perhaps a helping verb hanging out all alone. There is such a thing called a nominal sentence where you don't include a verb, but unless you are desperate to sound like an 18th-century English philosopher, I doubt you will ever have cause to use it.

The naming block: understanding nouns

Everyone deserves a name and boy do we have a lot of them! In fact, humankind is rather obsessed with naming everything! We have named the furthest star and the smallest of creatures found at the bottom of the ocean.

As names are so very important to us, you will see them coming up in nearly all the sentences that you write. The naming building block of language is called a noun. We will take a look at how nouns are identified now. What is key to keep in mind is that nouns can name anything including people, animals, places, things, and ideas.

My **dog** is small.

In this example, the noun is a **dog** who happens to be small. It is easy to find the noun is the case.

My **dog** is a **Chihuahua.**

However, in this example, there are two nouns. The first one is the **dog** and the second one is the **Chihuahua.** Very often, there is more than one noun in a sentence, remember what I said about our love of naming things.

You might notice that on one of the nouns there is no capitalization, whereas on the other there is. We will go into capitalization in detail further on in this book. For now, what I want you to know is that the reason **dog** is not capitalized is because it is considered a common noun. Common nouns are the names we give to everyday things that we talk about all the time. They might be cats, cars, cauliflowers, croissants, but they are not Christmas. That is because like **Chihuahua,** Christmas is a proper noun. These types of nouns have capital letters because they are not considered common and are talking about a specific thing. Remember it this way, a dog can be lots of different types of dogs but a Chihuahua can only ever be a Chihuahua. That is what is meant to be specific.

What is more, the two different nouns have two different functions in the sentence. Firstly, the noun **dog** is acting as the subject in the sentence. What this means is that the sentence is about the dog being a Chihuahua. It is not about any dog or any Chihuahua. It is specifically about it being that dog.

Secondly, the noun **Chihuahua** is acting as the object in the sentence. This is because the dog being talked about in the sentence is not just any dog, it is specifically a Chihuahua.

We just learned about verbs, and in this sentence, the verb is the helping verb **is.** If we then analyze the whole sentence, we can see that it is broken down into three main parts.

Subject + Verb + Object

My dog + is + a Chihuahua

This structure is a very common sentence structure that we use in English. However, I must admit that it can become a bit complicated to start to think about writing in terms of structure as well as having to consider using the different building blocks such as verbs and nouns. What is most important is to recognize how the majority of sentences should be written without worrying too much about what the different parts are called.

When writing, you have to write about something, this is what we call the subject. This something has to be doing something, this is what we call the verb. Then, the something doing something is probably doing something that has a name as well, this is what we call the object. So the something being talked about in this sentence is the dog. The dog is doing something and that is being something. What that dog is being is a Chihuahua.

You can apply this to lots of sentences you write to be able to understand if you are using your nouns correctly. Just check that you understand who is being talked about, that you know what they are doing and what the name is of what they are doing. Sounds simple, hey!

The replacing block: understanding pronouns

We just learned about how much we love naming things and what a noun is. So, what if I were to tell you that actually sometimes we don't want to name things and instead replace the actual name of something with a generic term that isn't at all descriptive or creative? Well, the answer is yes. Sometimes, we get a bit lazy. Scratch that, we often get pretty lazy and want to shorten our language so that we can quickly deliver the message of what we want to say.

Jessica and **Juan** walked across the road.

In this sentence, we can clearly see two proper nouns, **Jessica** and **Juan**, just as we have learned in the noun section of this book. Now, if we want to say this sentence more quickly, what would we write?

They walked across the road.

Very easily, we have replaced **Jessica** and **Juan** with **they.** By doing this, we have replaced the nouns with a pronoun.

Pronouns act just like nouns, they are a naming word. However, pronouns are a shortened version of a noun and replace the name. You will see pronouns in many sentences and we particularly use them when speaking. Pronouns include I, me, she, he, it, they, us, them, that, this and these. You can always spot a pronoun because it is not a specific name but if you wanted to you could replace it with a specific name.

She loves running.

Jessica loves running.

As you can see, **she** is easily replaced by **Jessica.** This shows you that it is a pronoun. The same goes if you are trying to work out whether you can replace a noun with a pronoun.

The **dog** is a **Chihuahua.**

It is a **Chihuahua.**

Returning to the example from before, the noun **dog** is easily replaced with the pronoun **it.** Yet, the proper noun **Chihuahua** can't be replaced with a pronoun as it would not make any sense.

It is an **it.**

As we love to speed up everything we do, you will come across pronouns very regularly. Feel free to use them to replace nouns. A word to the wise though, make sure that your reader knows what noun you are replacing it with. If you talk only about **it** and not the **dog**, the reader may never know you are talking about a dog. The best way is to mention the actual noun at the beginning of each new paragraph to make sure everyone understands what is going on.

The describing block: understanding adjectives

Life would be nothing if we couldn't say how much we love it or hate it! We are expressive creatives and we want to shout out to the world what we really think about something. To do this, we need to use the describing building blocks of the English language which are called adjectives.

Adjectives add depth and richness to your language. They are very important in transforming what you are writing from a simple non-descriptive sentence to one that packs a real punch! Adjectives are words used to describe both a noun and a pronoun.

The music is **loud**.

In this example, the adjective is **loud** because it is describing how the music is, which is a noun. We could also change the word **loud** and replace it with many other adjectives, such as melodic, beautiful, irritating, etc.

An adjective is put in a sentence when we want to answer a question about a noun. These questions are:

1. Which one?
2. What kind?
3. How many?
4. Whose?

Using the above example, if we were to ask the question of what kind of music is it? We would get the response, the music is **loud.** In this case, the kind of music being played is loud music. By being able to answer the above questions is what makes a word an adjective.

Something which can cause confusion when it comes to adjectives is that a noun can actually be an adjective in some cases.

Jessica's music is **enchanting.**

With this example, we are talking about music again and it is easy to identify that **enchanting** is an adjective as it answers the question of what kind of music? As well as **enchanting** being an adjective, so also is **Jessica's.** You might be thinking, hang on a second, the word Jessica is clearly a noun as it is naming a person. You are not wrong. However, with the addition of 's, Jessica becomes Jessica's which changes it to an adjective. This is because when you ask one of the adjective questions, whose? Jessica's is the answer to whose music it is?

Articles are the final piece of the adjective puzzle and something that quite a few people trip up over. Not to worry, follow the advice below and you will always be able to tell your a from your an. The good news is, though they are often misused, there are not very many of them to misuse. In English, there are three articles, the, a and an.

I want to eat **an** apple.

In this sentence, the person wants to eat **an** apple and it doesn't matter which one it is. This is because the person has not specified that they want to eat a specific apple. The word **an** is an adjective because it is describing the apple. It is also an indefinite article because it is not describing a specific apple.

I want to eat **the** apple.

In this example, you can see that the person is saying that they want to eat **the** apple and that apple is a very specific one. They won't eat just any old apple, it has to be the one they are talking about. Once again, the world **the** is an adjective because it is describing which apple. As well, it is also a definite article as it describes exactly which apple the person wants to eat.

As you can see, adjectives can take a few different forms. It can start to get a bit confusing so you must always remember that an adjective can only ever be describing a noun. Keep this in mind and you won't see yourself fall over by using them incorrectly.

The modifying block: understanding adverbs

Remember, when I said we love describing things, and when I said we love naming things, well we also love to go into lots of detail to make sure that we are absolutely understood. This is where adverbs come in. Adverbs are words that describe verbs, adjectives, and even other adverbs. Yes, it is true, when you thought an adjective was enough to describe something, you were wrong! In all seriousness, adverbs are super helpful building blocks that modify the words we are using to describe a situation so that understanding is clear.

My daughter is **extremely** polite.

As you can see, the sentence above demonstrates that the person has a daughter who is **extremely** polite. The word polite is an adjective and already describes the daughter as being polite. Yet, the world **extremely** describes how polite the daughter is, making it an adverb. The impact of the adverb upon the sentence becomes much clearer when you change the adverb for something else.

My daughter is **not** polite.

Now the situation being described has been reversed. Even though the adjective polite is still present in the sentence, the meaning is now changed to show that the daughter is anything but polite. The word **not** is an adverb and an important one to remember. That is because you are able to recognize adverbs easily because they almost all end in ly. However, one of the most commonly used adverbs is **not** and this doesn't follow the above rule.

Trying to identify adverbs is fairly simple as all you need to do is ask yourself the following questions about the verbs in your sentence:

1. How?
2. Where?
3. Why?
4. When?
5. To what extent?

These questions are crucial in sussing out what is an adverb as well as allowing you to understand how to add an adverb to a sentence.

We should eat dinner.

This example does not contain an adverb. It is currently demonstrating that a group of people should eat dinner. What dinner that is or where they will eat is unknown. However, if we do ask the question where they should eat, we can insert an adverb to make the sentence clearer.

We should eat dinner **there**.

The word **there** is clarifying exactly where they should eat dinner and this is what makes it an adverb. It describes the verb to eat as it is not just eating, it is eating **there**.

Finally, a really common way of using adverbs is to describe the different degrees of something. This misuse of this concept, called comparatives and superlatives, is hands down the most frequent mistake I see English speakers make. Let's dig into it to understand it further and help you to correct this mistake, fast!

That horse can run **quickly.**

In this example, the word **quickly** is an adverb describing the verb to run. If we change it a bit we can make it a comparative adverb.

That horse can run **more quickly** than other horses.

By adding **more** we have suggested that the horse can do

something to a greater degree than other horses. It is called a comparative adverb as we are comparing one thing to another, in this case, horses.

That horse can run the **most quickly** out of all horses.

Now we are saying that this horse can run quicker than any other horse. In this instance, the adverb is a superlative and it is stating that the thing we are talking about can do something to the highest degree possible.

Hang on a second, can't we also say:

That horse can run **quicker** than other horses.

Not to mention:

That horse can run the **quickest** out of all horses.

Yes, you are not wrong. The two examples above are both grammatically correct and do convey the same meaning as the other examples we have just gone through. However, they are not adverbs they are adjectives. This is something that people routinely forget.

How do you tell the difference? Well, a super quick way is to see if the word ends in ly or not. If it ends in ly then it is definitely an adverb. However, as we mentioned you can't always rely on all adverbs ending in ly. A better way to see what is what is to try and replace the verb in the sentence with **is.**

The horse is **more quickly**.

The horse is **quicker.**

If the sentence turns out grammatically correct, then you can be certain you are dealing with an adjective. Adverbs don't pair with the verb to be.

What is more, learn this quick trick to stop messing up your comparative and superlative adjectives. If the adjective has less than two beats to it, then you don't add the word more. If it has more than three, then you do.

1

Quick

This has one beat so to turn it into a comparative you add 'er' and to a superlative, you add 'est'.

Quicker and Quickest

But if it has three or more beats you can't do this.

1 - 2 - 3

Beau - ti - ful

In this case, you have to add 'more' to turn it into a comparative and 'most' to turn it into a superlative.

More beautiful and most beautiful

And with that, I think you should be there. You have just successfully navigated your way through all the essential building blocks of the English language. I have a lot more to teach you when it comes to truly master grammar, but even if you were to stop here and do nothing further, you would find that you are now far ahead of the rest of your peers in understanding how to use grammar correctly.

Don't stop here! We are going to move on now to understand even more grammatical concepts and work towards leveling up the way you write and speak. Remember to review this chapter a few times though. Even if you don't read it all, go through the examples and write your own. Pick up something you have recently written and check whether you put a verb in every sentence and if you correctly used nouns, adjectives, and adverbs. I am sure it will be illuminating as to your actual level of English grammar. Don't worry if you don't like what you find. We are going to be working on a significant improvement in every aspect of the way you use grammar going forward.

RULE 2 – FAMILIARIZE WITH KEY GRAMMAR COMPONENTS

How are you feeling? You have made it through rule number 1 (good job) and now we are striving towards rule number 2. Just a few things to remember before we proceed. This process of becoming a grammar genius is a quick one. The book is short for a reason so that you only have to learn exactly what you need to know to write flawlessly. We have made it accessible but that doesn't mean that you are going to absorb this information by osmosis. You need to work on it a little bit. Go through the examples as much as you can and understand each key component before moving onto the next.

If you think you have mastered your verbs, nouns, adjectives, and adverbs, well then come on in. Now we are going to talk about all the little words that go in between the important building block words we learned in the previous chapter. Like with most of the other grammatical rules that we have gone through so far, without these little words, we wouldn't have a language and we wouldn't be able to communicate. Which would be terrible. So let's make sure we know them.

Making connections: understanding conjunctions

Having words that show what we are doing, what we are feeling and what we have named something are all very well and good except when we can't join them up into actual sentences. This is why need conjunctions.

These little wonder words glue our words and phrases together into sentences that show meaning. When we start off simple, we might only have one conjunction in a sentence. As we progress further, you will find yourself using multiple conjunctions in one sentence to produce complex sentence structures. That is why we need to make sure we understand how to use them properly from the very beginning.

Today, I went swimming **and** running.

The word **and** is the most common conjunction in the English language and you can probably understand why. We very rarely want to say just one thing. More often than not, we want to say lots of things. To do this we need to have a word that connects one thing we want to say with another thing we want to say that is related to the first thing. How we do that is by using **and.**

There are a ton of different conjunctions that we can use to bring meaning to our sentences by connecting information together, but there are only three main types.

The first type is conjoining conjunctions. The best way to remember these ones is that they glue together words that are related together.

I want to buy a dress **or** a coat.

The conjunction here is **or** because it is connecting two similar parts together, one part about wanting to buy a dress and one about wanting to buy a coat. What is important is that this conjunction specifies that I want to buy only one, not both. If we changed the conjunction to another conjoining conjunction it would change the meaning of the sentence.

I want to buy a dress **and** a coat.

This sentence shows that I want to buy both items. By simply changing the conjunction in this sentence, I have completely changed the meaning. This shows you the power of conjunctions.

The next type of conjunctions are subordinating conjunctions. These words also help to show a connection between two different phrases but they are different in that they connect two phrases, one that can stand alone as a sentence and one that can't.

I want to go to Spain **because** of the weather.

Because is the most common subordinating conjunction and clearly shows that you want to do something because of something else. Also, as you can see, I want to go to Spain is a complete sentence but of the weather is not. The conjunction **because** is essential in establishing meaning in this case.

Since I was a child, I have wanted to go to Spain.

Subordinating conjunctions can also appear at the beginning of sentences. What is more, they are very often about time. In this sentence, the conjunction **since** indicates that you have wanted to go to Spain since childhood. Without it there, the sentence would not have any meaning.

The last type of conjunction is correlative conjunctions. These are different because they always come in pairs. They are also very useful to use and can raise your writing level. They act in the same way as conjoining conjunctions in that they add words and phrases together.

Both Jessica **and** Juan crossed the road.

This example clearly demonstrates that two people crossed the road with the use of the conjunction **both** and the conjunction **and** in a pair. It is a useful device to use correlative conjunctions as it makes certain that no other meaning could be understood from this sentence. When we write anything, having another person understand exactly what we mean is the ultimate goal.

It is clear that we can't do without conjunctions when we speak. They are the literal glue of the English language and allow us to be really clear in what we are saying.

Making relationships: understanding prepositions

When we have a group of words that might be a combination of verbs, nouns, adjectives, and adverbs, they are trying to form some sort of meaning together but to do this they need a little help. What these types of words lack is the ability to show how they relate to other words or phrases properly. This is where prepositions come in. A preposition is usually a small word that is inserted into the sentence to demonstrate a relationship between a noun and some other word in the sentence.

Jessica crossed the road **with** Juan.

In this example, the word **with** is the preposition as it demonstrates the relationship between Jessica and Juan in that they crossed the road together.

The horse ran the race **despite** having an injury.

This is another example to show that there is a range of different prepositions and that the placing of them in the sentence is really important. In this sentence, the meaning is demonstrating that the horse did something **despite** something else. The first thing, running the race, has a direct relationship to the second thing, having an injury, because of the preposition **despite.**

You could write this example as two different sentences but the relationship between the two phrases would not be made clear.

The horse ran the race. The horse has an injury.

As you can see, the impact and meaning have been lost. This shows the importance of prepositions in establishing an understanding of what is really trying to be said.

Another important thing to understand about prepositions is that they don't always appear where you expect them to be, yet this does not affect the sentence's meaning.

The dog is **behind** the chair.

Behind the chair is the dog.

These two sentences mean exactly the same thing and are both grammatically correct. However, I would suggest that to make certain your intended meaning is conveyed correctly, that you try to insert prepositions in the middle of a sentence. Think about what thing you want to relate to another thing and write two simple sentences about them. Now take a preposition and try to insert it in the middle to make a complex sentence.

I studied math. I went to high school.

I studied math **throughout** high school.

These two sentences have been combined to show that you not only studied maths but that you studied it **throughout** your time at high school.

There is quite a large list of prepositions and sometimes people forget which is one and which isn't one. The number one rule to remember, if you can't connect two simple sentences together with the word then it won't be a preposition. All prepositions show a relationship between the words and phrases.

Making it shorter: understanding abbreviations

So far in this chapter, we have gone through a whole bunch of little words that literally help us to make sense of our language and communicate clearly. We really couldn't do without them. However, there does exist a whole category of tiny words that are not the result of wanting to be clearer in our language, rather they have come from the desire to be faster. These are abbreviations which are shortened versions of words that we commonly use.

As I have previously said, the way we use the English language can sometimes be a bit contradictory. Sometimes, we are obsessed with making certain that the meaning of what we are trying to say is translated correctly. This leads us to use grammatical rules to ensure clarity. Then, on the other hand, we also like to speak quickly but still convey meaning. The truth is, there is a time and place for both styles of English language use. For example, being grammatically correct and using well thought out sentence structures is essential for the formal use of the English language. Whereas, using devices such as abbreviations where we shorten words despite compromising understanding, is much more suited to informal language use. So, before I demonstrate abbreviations, just remember that if you are trying to up your formal language game, then you should use them lightly, particularly in written work.

That being said, abbreviations can be really useful in quickly conveying a message. Many of them have also become so common that we are much more accustomed to hearing the abbreviation than we are the full version of the word or phrase.

Dr. Ramirez is ready to see you.

The word doctor, in this case, is very commonly abbreviated to **Dr.** with a period placed after the abbreviation. It would be odd for us to see it written out as Doctor Ramirez as this abbreviation is now the accepted norm.

FYI there is a letter for you at reception.

This abbreviation is an acronym, meaning it has taken the first letter of each word in the phrase to form it. **FYI** means for your information. It is frequently seen in emails between staff members and on social media messaging sites. However, it is also a clear example of informal language and therefore must only be used informally. Writing it in a memo to your boss is certainly not the best way to impress.

N.B. classes will start at 10 am next week.

The final group of acronyms that do make their way into formal language are those which have come from Latin, then abbreviated and subsequently used by a majority of those in academia, which in turn have made them common in all formal writing. **N.B.** means *nota bene* which translates as take note. **E.g.** means *exempli gratia* which translates as for example. Finally, **etc.** means *et cetera* which translates as so on. All of these examples, you will have come across and will continue to see. My advice is to use them sparingly to avoid any confusion. It is simple enough to say for example so why use e.g.?

As I have made obvious, abbreviations can be a bit of a double-edged sword. Yes, they may save you time and lots of people may be familiar with them. However, on the whole, writing out the words in full or using a comparable phrase is preferable. Being clear and concise so someone else can understand should always be favored over speed.

Making it obvious: understanding interjections

Oh! Are you paying attention? Wow! I thought you had fallen asleep there for a minute. Hang on! Let's turn this up a notch.

Are you wondering what is going on? Well, what is going on is that I had a sudden rush of strong emotions and wanted to convey this to you through the written word. To do this, I used a little word that makes a big impact called an interjection.

Yikes! I am going to be late.

In this example, **yikes** is an example of an interjection as it is a word that is usually only spoken but has been written down to maximize the impact upon the reader. Saying I am going to be late only shows to the reader that you are late. Whereas with the addition of **yikes**, you have made it clear that you are worried that you are going to be late and feel strongly about it.

It is obvious that, as with abbreviations, interjections live mainly in the world of informal language. That being said, they can be useful when writing creatively as they certainly pack a punch and convey a meaning that you wouldn't get if you didn't use one.

Wow! I didn't expect to get an A on my English paper.

Strong, emotive words are almost all interjections, including **wow, ouch, aww, eww, help!** It also follows, because of the strength of the words, that they also include an exclamation mark after them. They are certainly useful for getting over the right impact but as with abbreviations, it is certainly wise to use them sparingly in your written work. Save the strong emotions for your friends and family. It is always best to impress your literature professor with the elegance of your language rather than the force of it.

Bravo! You have made it to the end of rule 2. Not only have you conquered verbs, nouns, adjectives, and adverbs, but you also know how to put them together with useful little connecting words that are essential for structuring a grammatically correct sentence. Don't forget to check out the examples a few more times to check that you really do know your stuff.

RULE 3 – THE FOUR H'S: HOMONYMS, HOMPHONES, HOMOGRAPHS AND HETERONYMS

It is great to see you here at rule 3! We have made it this far together already. Now is the time to dig deep and push through the rest of the chapters. Believe me, this is where it gets exciting.

Before we start, I think I should let you in on a little secret. Well, less of a secret and more of a confession. So here goes. English isn't actually a very logical language and it does its best at all times to confuse and terrify speakers of it! The truth is, as it has developed over time, and incorporated rules from German, French, and other languages, it has managed to confuse itself. English has often been called the language of exception because it can feel as if it has more exceptions to the rules than instances of actually following that rule. To be fair, that isn't actually true. Lots of the English language is logical. It is just here and there, there exist some rather infuriating diversions away from the central rules.

So, when we go through the rest of this book together, and you feel a burning desire to question me on why what I am explaining is not always logical, well it isn't. However, it is the way that it is. What I mean, is despite the confusing nature of English grammar, it has been standardized and therefore we are able to learn how to use it correctly. Don't sweat it too much, if you can enjoy the uneven path of English grammar, you will then certainly become a master of it.

This brings me swiftly on to the 4 H's which are homonyms, homophones, homographs, and heteronyms. The 4 H's are tricky little beasts but also very enjoyable to learn. So let's dive in.

Homonyms - the same sound and the same spelling

The group of words called homonyms is defined as words that

sound the same and are spelled the same but have different meanings. You might think about why we couldn't just come up with new spellings or different words entirely to describe them. Well, we didn't and that is why you need to learn how to correctly interpret the meaning of the sentence.

I went to the country **fair** to meet a **fair** maiden with **fair** skin where we enjoyed the rides for a very **fair** price.

When you read the word **fair** in this sentence you should pronounce it exactly the same way each time. As you can see, the spelling is also identical each time. This means that **fair** is a homonym. Each example of the world **fair** used in the sentence has a different meaning. A country **fair** is a type of festival. A **fair** maiden is a beautiful woman. **Fair** skin means light skin and a **fair** price means reasonably priced.

Let's try another example. These are fun!

Well, now that you are **well** I can fetch water from

the **well**.

Once again, we have three different versions of a word, with the same spelling and same sound that all mean different things. **Well** at the beginning of the sentence is an exclamation showing that something is about to happen. Now that you are **well** means now that you are feeling better. Fetch water from the **well** is a location where water can be found.

When you see homonyms in a sentence you need to pay attention to the other words around it to be certain that you understand it. If you get confused with its meaning, work out whether it is a noun or an adjective, or perhaps something else. This will give you clues to what it really means.

When it comes to writing yourself, think about how you use homonyms in a sentence. Having a clear meaning is essential when writing. So, if too many homonyms are going to confuse your reader, try and swap one of them out for a different word that means the same thing.

Homophones - the same sound with a different spelling

There is only really one example that we need to talk about when we go through what a homophone is (don't worry, we will actually go through three!) As soon as I mention it, you will know what I am referring to. A homophone is a group of words that all sound the same but have a different spelling. They also represent the most repeated mistake that a native speaker of English will make when writing. Let's see that first example now so we can all get on the same page.

You're behaving exactly like **your** brother, naughty and rude!

The misuse of **your** and **you're** is widespread among all native speakers of English. Are you guilty of it? Don't worry if you are, we will fix it now. So to be very clear, **you're** is a contracted version of the two words 'you are'. **Your** is a possessive word that means something belongs to you, in this case, it is your brother.

What most people do who confuse the meaning of these two homophones, is use only **your** in all circumstances.

Your very welcome!

I am sure you have seen this common mistake, perhaps someone has ridiculed you for making it yourself. To make sure that you don't make it again when writing, slow down a bit and think about what it is you are trying to say. You are very welcome is the correct and full version of this sentence. If you want to shorten it, you can to **you're.** My advice though, if you don't want to mess up while writing, use the full version every time.

Their new house is over **there** and **they're** really pleased to be in this neighborhood.

Very similarly to the previous example, many people trip up over this homophone. Let's clear it up together. **Their** is a possessive word and means that something is theirs. It will always have a noun after it, in this case, it is their new house.

There is a location word meaning that over there. **They're** is a contracted word meaning they are. Just like before, if you don't know which version to use, slow down and think of the meaning. If you can avoid using they're you will also find that you don't fall in the trap that it has laid for you.

Homographs - the same spelling and the same sound

Yes, you may be thinking what is the difference between a homograph which has the same spelling and the same sound and a homonym that has the same sound and the same spelling? Your question is very valid. The truth is, there is not much of a difference between them other than what is considered important to a homonym is that they sound the same. But with a homograph what is considered important is that it has the same spelling. If after this chapter, you are still not sure about the difference between them, don't worry about it. Instead, focus on practicing the examples because they are what will show you how to use each word correctly.

Your **lie** has upset me so much, I have to go **lie** down.

In this example, the spelling is the same and the words sound the same but both have very different meanings. The first **lie** means to be deceived by someone and it is a noun. The second **lie** means to lay down on the bed, and this is a verb. When you see these words, you can figure out which one is which by recognizing which one is the noun and which one is the verb.

Heteronyms - the same spelling with a different sound

The final one of our 4 H's is the mighty heteronym. This group of words all have the same spelling but have a different sound. As a native English speaker, you have a bit of an advantage that you intuitively know how to pronounce these words. You can imagine that if you are approaching English as a second or third language, it can be pretty tricky to explain that they are spelled the same but are not spoken in the same way. They are absolutely one of the many exceptions that we have in the English language, in this case, they are an exception based on what is considered a standardized vowel sound. You should be able to approach any language and given that you understand the way the vowels are pronounced in combination with other letters, work out how to pronounce it. English just doesn't work this way. Unless someone shows you the different pronunciations, you could continue to say it incorrectly until someone does.

Luckily, when it comes to writing, you don't need to worry about how a word is pronounced, you only need to worry about using it correctly.

I put down my **bow** and took a **bow.**

In this example, to identify what is what with these two homographs, you need to see which word is the noun and which word is the verb. The first **bow** is a noun, which we can see because it has the possessive word my before it. This **bow** means a violin bow that is used to play the instrument. It could also be a bow and arrow but because the rest of the sentence is about **bowing** to an audience, you can assume it is talking about the instrument and not a weapon! The second **bow** is about bending your back to accept congratulations from an audience.

When I **graduate** I will become a **graduate.**

This example is very useful as it demonstrates how a verb and a noun of the same word route are pronounced differently. In this sentence, the first **graduate** is a verb meaning when you matriculate from college. The second **graduate** is a noun meaning you will be a person with a degree. These two words are heteronyms of each other because they are spelled the same but sound different. This is very common with lots of verb/noun combinations of the same word route. For example, insult, abuse, contest, permit, etc.

A really helpful way to remember how to pronounce these words is to learn the correct intonation for both the verb and the noun. When it is the verb version of the world the intonation is placed on the second beat of the word. In **graduate,** this means that 'duate is emphasized. Whereas, with the noun version, the first beat is emphasized, which in this case is gra'. Try this out with the different words listed above and you will see that this formula works every time!

So there we go, you have just had your first introduction into the wonderful world of the exceptions of the English language. If you are anything like me, you will enjoy these little idiosyncrasies. If you are not, don't worry, just set about learning them thoroughly so you're not laughed out of the board meeting for putting 'your welcome' in your Powerpoint presentation!

RULE 4 – BECOME A PUNCTUATION PRO

I want to write a really clear chapter for you that explains exactly why punctuation is key because without punctuation we would be faced with incredibly long sentences that never seem to end or have any direction to them instead they simply continue onwards until some cataclysmic event stops them or perhaps the cat comes to sit on the laptop forcing the writer to pay attention to the cat wanting to have dinner rather than focusing on how to form a punchy punctuation chapter that inspires people to use punctuation correctly which whilst the writer pauses to think about the cat at that moment fortunately puts its tail on the period button.

Wow! That was uncomfortable, wasn't it? That is because life without punctuation is uncomfortable as it simply loses meaning and we are unable to communicate effectively.

Think of punctuation as the conductor in an orchestra. As part of an orchestra, you have the strings section, the brass section, the percussion section, and the wind section. These represent our verbs, nouns, adjectives, and adverbs. If all of these sections were to play at once, or in an unorganized way, the sound they would make would be terrible. Enter center stage, the conductor. The function of this person is to manage all of the different sections and organize them so they play at different times and for different reasons. The result is a beautiful, melodic piece of music.

The same goes for punctuation. It serves as a way to organize our written language so that the reader knows where one sentence starts and where another one begins. As well as this, different forms of punctuation can be used to emphasize certain parts of the sentence, such as an exclamation mark which indicates surprise or shock to the reader.

So rather than having long, rambling sentences about your cat, learn how to become a punctuation pro and you will certainly impress with your writing skills.

Know when to end it: understanding periods, question marks and exclamation marks

All great things must come to an end, even your new and improved written work. However, finishing sentences off correctly is something that English speakers are not particularly good at. If you don't pay attention to grammar, you will easily find yourself writing as if you are speaking. The result of this is you often sound like you are babbling. You must be concise with your written language and this is why punctuation is your savior.

That being said, before we start on this punctuation journey, I want to make a suggestion that you learn how to use punctuation sparingly. Don't stuff your sentences full with punctuation just because you know how to use it. Short, well-written sentences always beat long, convoluted structures. Keep it simple and you can't go wrong.

I went to the shop.

This sentence is as simple as it gets. We have a pronoun, a verb, and a noun followed by a period. As is with all sentences, the period is placed at the very end to suggest to the reader that we have finished explaining one piece of information.

I went to the shop. I wanted to buy some bread.

I went to the shop as I wanted to buy some bread.

These two examples have exactly the same meaning, yet one is said in two sentences and the other in one. When using a period, you can join two related sentences together with a conjunction followed by placing a period at the end of both now newly joined sentences. We will go further into detail later on about phrases and clauses, but what is important to understand at this stage is that you can join up similar information into one sentence. If it isn't similar or related, then put it in two.

How much does the bread cost**?**

Another way to end a sentence is with a question mark. As the name suggests, you use a question mark when you are asking a question. Remember, to ask a question, you also have to use one of the question words, which are how, why, what, when, where, and who.

We have an incredible offer on bread today**!**

This is an example of using an exclamation mark. It is used this way to draw the reader's attention towards an exciting offer on bread. If you were to say this sentence, you would almost certainly put a lot of energy into it. You would probably raise your voice a bit and open your mouth wide. This is because you want to make an impact with the sentence as most likely you want people to be excited and come and buy your bread. When it comes to writing, you can't guarantee that a reader will understand the emotion you intend behind a sentence, so putting an exclamation mark at the end can indicate that this sentence has a strong meaning and conveys your intended emotion.

Get away from my house, now!

As you can see in this example, an exclamation mark can show more than one emotion. It is not limited to showing a happy emotion. In this case, the sentence is demonstrating anger and fear. By placing the exclamation mark at the end, it allows the reader to feel the urgency of what is being said.

You know I like to throw in a caveat or two. Well, there is a caveat with exclamation marks that is you don't want to overuse them. Though they are excellent at conveying emotion, outside of the world of creative writing and sales, they can make your writing seem immature. Used sparingly, they are much more impactful than packing every other sentence with them.

Know when to take a break: understanding commas

Where a period is a definite end to a sentence, a comma is

more like taking a break. You never know you might get back together after it. In all seriousness, commas are very useful for breaking up your written language and emphasizing meaning. You can look at a comma as a small pause between related information in a sentence. Some people equate it to taking a breath while speaking. I prefer to see it as a device for making the meaning of the sentence clearer.

However, the misuse of commas is an epidemic among English speakers. The reason is, as I said above, people believe that commas act in the same way as pausing while speaking. The problem with this is that people speak in largely different ways. Some people speak really quickly, going through tons of information in a very short time. Then you find people who speak very slowly, gently meandering through what they are trying to say. It often follows, that if you are a faster talker then you will tend to use very few commas and instead pack your sentences with conjunctions. On the other side of the spectrum, slow speakers stuff their sentences with commas rather than ending them and starting a new sentence. Either way, both strategies result in comma abuse.

You saw at the start of this chapter an example of not using a comma correctly. The result was a very long and uncomfortable to read sentence that has no place in being in a grammar book. That being said, if we had broken that sentence up with commas only, it still would have been far too long. The number one rule of commas is to join up similar pieces of information. If it is not related, start a new sentence. Don't worry if you are unsure at this point in time about how to tell what is and isn't related. We are going to run through all the different ways of using a comma to make it really clear.

After school, I am going to meet my friend Jessica.

This is an example of using a comma after an introductory phrase. **After school** is the introductory phrase and can't be a sentence by itself because it doesn't have a verb. By placing a comma after the phrase, it allows the reader to be certain that the person is going to meet their friend Jessica after school rather than just in general.

My mother, I was happy to see, was feeling much better.

Commas can also be used to break up sentences that contain information that is non-essential but placed within the sentence to show emotion. This method uses commas as interpreters in the sentence by surrounding the non-essential information. In this example, **I was happy to see** is considered non-essential information but something that adds value to the sentence. Therefore it has a comma placed before it and after it.

That was really scary, wasn't it?

Another way of using a comma is to place it just before asking a question. In this example, the comma is placed before asking, **wasn't it?** The question at the end is called a question tag. It is a fairly informal way of asking a question so it is best restricted to informal written work. To change it to be formal, write it as **do you agree that it was really scary?**

Adam, there is a person waiting for you at reception.

Whenever you address a person directly in a sentence, you

need to include a comma directly after their name. More often than not, you will place the name at the beginning of the sentence as you are usually giving them some sort of direction.

My father, Juan, is an incredible singer.

This is an example of a nonessential appositive where you use commas to separate similar information. What this means in lay terms is that **my father** and **Juan** represent the same information told differently as it is talking about the same person but using a different name to describe them. It is a nonessential appositive because you could remove either **my father** or **Juan** from the sentence and it would still make sense.

William Shakespeare's play *A Midsummer Night's Dream* is a fine example of classical theatre.

This sentence contains an essential appositive which is not separated by commas. That is because the title of the play is essential information. If you removed it from the sentence, you would not be able to understand which of William Shakespeare's plays is being talked about. So the trick to knowing whether you use commas is to see what happens when you take out one of the nouns which refer to the same thing. Does the sentence still make sense? Great, use commas to separate that word out from the rest of the sentence.

> March 3, 2009, is an important day in the history of the company as we won our first major client.

When it comes to putting commas around dates, we are a bunch of very confused writers! Do we put the comma before the day, the month, the year? What if we change the format of the date, does that affect it? I think we need to clear this up once and for all.

When you write the date in month-day-year format, like the example above, you need to use commas after the day and the year. If you are writing it in day-month-year format then commas are not necessary. It can be a bit tricky to remember this rule, so my suggestion is that you say the date out loud. When you say March 3, 2009, out loud you automatically pause between the day and the year. If you say 3 March 2009 out loud you will notice that you don't pause. Therein lies the trick.

That woman is an aggressive, self-righteous, offensive hypocrite.

Now we come on to the good stuff. We love to list all of the ways that people both delight and annoy us in equal measures. Listing is something that most people are aware of as needing commas to separate out the different items. However, when it comes to adjectives, you must be careful to not put a comma in where it shouldn't be. In the above example, all of the adjectives being used could be said in any order and still make sense. Therefore, you use commas to split them up.

The charming little girl came by the house again.

Whereas, in this example, you can't interchange the words charming and little. Therefore, this means that you don't need to use any commas but the word order must remain the same.

Jessica could have been an actress, but she didn't want to leave home.

Another way to use a comma is before the word **but**. Be careful with this one though, it feels natural to pause before saying the word but. However, you only add a comma before it when the phrase after it is an independent clause, meaning it could be a sentence all by itself.

I love oranges but hate lemons.

This is an example of when the phrase after the **but** couldn't be a sentence by itself. Therefore, you don't need to use a comma.

One more common mistake with commas is using the word **and.** In American English, people frequently place a comma before the word **and** mistakenly. The only instance that you use a comma with **and** is in a list. Take a look at this example for the correct use.

I went to the shop and bought bread, cheese, and chocolate.

If you notice in this example there are three items listed. That is why we have put a comma before the **and.** If there are only two items in a list, you don't need to use a comma. In fact, using a comma before an **and** in a list is entirely optional. So don't worry if you don't use one. The important thing is to not put in a comma when it shouldn't be there.

"It is fantastic to see you here!" said Juan.

"I like to eat jam on my toast," said Jessica.

These two examples show you when you should use a comma in quotation marks. The first example ends in an exclamation mark and is an instance in which you don't use a comma inside the quotation mark. The exclamation is important in the reader's understanding of the emphasis of this sentence which is why it is there and not replaced with a comma. The second example, however, does use a comma because this sentence would normally end with a period. You simply replace it the period with a comma and end the entire sentence with the period instead.

> After buying the candy (and promptly eating a few on the way over here), I gave them to my delighted grandmother.

In our final example of using commas correctly (yes, there are a lot), we can see how to use a comma correctly with parentheses. Whatever the situation, you don't use a comma before opening parenthesis, but you do use one after closing parenthesis before carrying on with the rest of the sentence.

So, there you have it! If you take a moment to learn how to use commas in different situations I can guarantee that you will be miles ahead of your colleagues when it comes to writing skills. They are so often misused that by doing it right you will shine bright!

Know when to separate: understanding colons, semicolons, hyphens, and dashes

We are going to move on to a group of punctuation now that in the 21st century have run away with themselves a little bit. This group of punctuation, which includes colons, semicolons, hyphens, and dashes, mainly live in the realm of informal language. That being said, they did start off their lives as formal punctuation and if we try really hard collectively, we may be able to restore them to their former glory.

Colons, semicolons, hyphens, and dashes are predominantly about emphasis. Their purpose is to amplify the meaning of what is about to be said. Nowadays, we write in very different ways depending on the context. If we are at work or college using emails and writing papers, we write very formally. If we are speaking with our friends and family over social media or through SMS, we tend to write informally. In the latter, we love to imbue what we are writing with the emotions we are feeling. Emotive language and informal grammatical structures have become very common because of the frequency with which we are using social media and SMS. This, in turn, has transferred to our formal written language, and in particular, we now regularly use colons and dashes, whereas in different eras they didn't see the light of day.

There are three different types of birds living by the lake: heron, starling, and blackbird.

Starting with colons, the main purpose of a colon is to alert the reader to important information in the sentence. In this case, the names of the birds are the essential information in the sentence. The colon is placed right before the list of birds and importantly it does not have a verb before it.

The three different types of birds living by the lake are heron, starling, and blackbird.

This example means exactly the same as above but it is written without a colon. That is because the word **are** has been placed before the list of bids and that is a verb. When you use a colon instead of a verb, in the mind of the reader they assume that you are saying the verb which is why it isn't needed.

You have two choices here: blonde and curly, or brunette and straight.

What comes after a colon doesn't have to be a list. It simply has to be related information. In this example, two choices are presented to the reader with the inference being that they must choose one option.

A bat is not a bird: it is a small mammal.

As you can see with this example, a colon has been placed between two pieces of related information. Each of these bits of information could be a separate sentence by themselves. By using a colon, the emphasis is placed on the bat being a mammal rather than a bird, for which it is commonly mistaken. The colon draws additional attention to this fact as if it is a big arrow pointing towards the second phrase that says don't forget this!

Keep this image of a big arrow with flashy lights in your head when you are using a colon. If the information that comes after a colon is not worthy of such attention, simply put a period and start a new sentence. 99% of the time, you should use a period over a colon. The 1% normally comes in titles as a colon can be a good way to create a catchy title that also includes an understandable explanation about what the reader is about to read.

I ordered an extra-large portion of fries; life is too short for counting calories.

Now we move on to the younger brother of the colon: the semicolon. Never has a punctuation mark been as controversial as the semicolon. The reason is that it has a reputation for being unnecessary and only used by those in high levels of academia. Neither is strictly true. There are plenty of legitimate reasons to use a semicolon over other punctuation. Nonetheless, if you use it incorrectly (or maybe even when you use it correctly), you may face a bit of stick for it. Unfairly so, but you have been given fair warning.

In the example above (and also a life mantra), you can see that a semicolon has been used to separate two complete sentences that are related to each other. A simple way to use a semicolon is to take two sentences and see if you can join them with a conjunction. If you can, whip that conjunction out of there and replace it with a semicolon.

> I need to order the following items: extra-large leggings; a dress with a zipper down the side; two pairs of size 8 red shoes; and a cheeseburger because I am still hungry!

Another useful way to use semicolons is when you are writing a list of items that have more than one word. The semicolon helps to pause the reader and identify which parts of the sentence belong to each list item. For example, a dress with a zip down the side is a long description. Having a semicolon after it rather than a comma serves to slow the reader down and ensure they understand exactly what the list item was before moving on.

What is her problem with me; moreover, why does she continue to insult me?

You can also use a semicolon to connect two sentences in which the second sentence starts with a conjunctive adverb such as more moreover, however, finally, likewise, etc. This is actually a pretty nifty way to punctuate such sentences as using such adverbs as above usually indicates that you are writing something emotional. Therefore, using a semicolon to emphasize the second part of the sentence is a great way to really assert the meaning.

This is a child-friendly restaurant.

Welcome to the world of hyphens, designed to trip you up! Don't worry it isn't that much to get your head around, it is just that we so commonly use the hyphen incorrectly that you will probably think the incorrect use is actually the right way to do it. The best thing to do is to clear your mind of everything you know about hyphens and let's start again with them from the beginning.

In the example above, a hyphen has been placed between the two words child and friendly to emphasize that they are connected in meaning. This is important as you must not understand the sentence as it being anything other than child-friendly. If these two words are separated you run the risk of the sentence being misinterpreted.

Juan has become a highly respected professor.

In contrast to the other example, this one does not use a hyphen. This is because even though highly and respected must be said in that order to preserve the correct meaning and that they are connected together, you do not use a hyphen when the first word is an adverb. How do you remember what is and isn't an adverb? If you recall, most adverbs end in 'ly. If you place a hyphen between these two words you will fall into the trap that many of us have before. Keep in mind, noun + adverb = hyphen, adverb + noun = no-hyphen. The reason behind this is that you could remove highly from the sentence without much impact on the meaning as adverbs are about a degree of something. So Juan would still be respected regardless. However, if you removed child from the other example, the restaurant would just be friendly, which is a bit weird; not to mention, it totally changes the meaning.

All students must read pages 10-19 of the coursebook.

When is a hyphen not a hyphen? Well, when it is a dash. Yes, they may look the same but they have very subtle differences in size and more importantly, they function differently. Have you ever experienced your word processor acting a little bit strange when you enter a hyphen between two words and all of a sudden the size of the hyphen gets bigger? Well, that is because your computer knows a thing or two about grammar and has actually inserted either an em dash or an en dash rather than a hyphen.

The example of the student's reading homework contains an en dash. It is a fairly simple device that places a dash instead of saying to or through. You can use this for numbers or time. It is very common to see it used as a shorthand. Just make sure you are using it for a range of numbers or a span of time. It is not for connecting random numbers together.

The Grammy Award-winning singer Jessica will be with us here tonight!

Another use of the en dash is to join together a two-word compound noun with an adjective to create a compound adjective. Jessica is not just a singer, she is a Grammy Award-winning singer. The en dash provides added emphasis to this in the sentence.

I always loved Dolly Parton - or rather, I was obsessed with her.

The dash in this sentence is different. It is called an em dash and can be used for emphasis as well. Notice that it has spaces either side of it, this is one way to tell what it is. In this sentence, the em dash is replacing parentheses. The reason is to exaggerate the information in the second part of the sentence, rather than side-lining it by placing it in parentheses. Once again though, this grammatical tactic can make your written work look a little bit immature and informal. One or two em dashes can impressive. Yet, a whole bunch of them looks like you are screaming all over the page!

He has always been allergic to two things: tomatoes and dairy.

He has always been allergic to two things - tomatoes and dairy.

In our final example of dashes, this is another em dash. It works in exactly the same way as a colon with the added oomph that an em dash provides. As with all our previous examples of separating out words using colons, semicolons, hyphens, and dashes, it is to be used lightly. Sprinkle a few into your work but don't overdo it. That way you can show that you really are a punctuation pro.

Know when to divide and conquer: understanding apostrophes

The apostrophe is a multitalented punctuation mark. It can

own everything and cut you out of the deal in an instant. Confused, don't worry. I will explain what I mean right now.

I am very excited for my sister's wedding.

First off let's talk about owning it all. To do that you need an apostrophe as it is the most common method to show possession, meaning that you or someone else owns something. In the example above, the person is excited about going to their sister's wedding. We know it is the wedding of their sister because there is an 's after the word sister.

You will be pleased to know that in English, there is only one way to show that something is possessive and that is to add an 's. So as long as you add this, you won't go too wrong.

I am very excited about my sister Jessica's wedding.

That being said, you may falter off track when trying to position the possessive when a few more words are added to the mix. In the above example, the possessive apostrophe has switched to the word Jessica and is no longer on the word sister. That is because it wouldn't make sense to stay on the word sister as it would suggest that the sister owns Jessica rather than Jessica owning her wedding. If you get confused, say it out loud and you will probably catch the mistake. Concentrate on who owns who.

This isn't anything to do with you.

Now comes the taking everything away from you part - or rather, taking everything away from the words. The above example showcases apostrophes being used in contractions. As you have heard me say before, we love to speed up our language. This has resulted in us shortening two words into one and using a contraction apostrophe to fill in the gaps. The word isn't is a contraction of is not.

There are lots of examples of contractions that we use regularly, such as don't, you're, hasn't, I'd, etc. Despite using them frequently, we all have a tendency to mess them up a bit and put the apostrophe in the wrong place. More often than not the apostrophe is placed before the last letter replacing vowel sounds in the second word. Commonly, people place it between the two contracted words, for example, do'nt and would'nt. Remember, the apostrophe is meant to replace missing letters so in the case of don't it is replacing the o in not.

There we are, it's finally time to leave.

The dog thinks its bed is the sofa.

As we wrap up apostrophes, it's about time we solved the ultimate apostrophe mystery: what is the difference between **it's** and **its**. You know that English is the language of exception and this is no exception, well, except it is an exception! When coming to deciding how to deal with the case of **it's** and **its**, it was a bit tricky for grammar theorists. The words it is had long been shortened to **it's** and so was already in common usage. However, **it** is a pronoun that can have a possessive and if it followed the possessive rule should add 's to the end of it. However, **it's** was already taken as a contraction so it was finally settled that **its** was to be used as the possessive. To work out which to use, ask yourself does the sentence say it is something or is it talking about owning something. Once you answer this, you will know the correct form to use.

Know when to wrap it up: understanding quotation marks and parentheses

As we come to the end of our journey through punctuation we are going to finish off with two superstars! First, let's discuss how we use quotation marks correctly. Second, we will wrap up the whole chapter with a how-to-guide on parentheses.

"The weather is going to be perfect in Marbella," Jessica said.

Quotation marks don't take much explaining. They are used whenever you insert someone else's words into your writing. The absolute rule of quotation marks is that when you open a set, you also have to close them. So, if you want to quote someone, you start with one set of quotation marks that point towards the right followed by the other person's words ending with a punctuation mark such as a comma and a second set of quotation marks that point towards the left.

> Juan contradicted Jessica, "They told me at the airport there would be a big storm in Marbella."

Another thing to keep in mind when using quotation marks is the position they come in the sentence. It is easier with the first example as it comes at the beginning. However, if it comes in the middle or end of a sentence you must remember to capitalize the first word in the quote.

"I think you will find I am right," said Jessica, "after all, I am the meteorologist."

That being said, if you decide to split your quote into two parts, you only capitalize the first letter of the first word in the first section of the quote, ending that section with a comma. When you add the second section of the quote, you don't need to capitalize it. When you are using this type of construction, think of it as one long quote that if written as a whole wouldn't have a random capital letter in the middle. That way you won't forget about the capitalization rule.

> At this time of year, you can hear recitations of Charles Dickens's 'A Christmas Carol' all across the city.

We can also use quotation marks to highlight the name of a short story, chapter or article in text. To do this, you can use only one quotation mark rather than two to indicate that it is not a direct quote. Be careful with this though as it is commonly misused. Using double quotation marks around the word or phrase is bad practice. It is called air quotes and is only used in media for emphasis. On the whole, it is better to italicize names and translations to highlight them. Any name of a book, film or famous person should never be put in quotes. However, if you stick to the italic format in your word processor, you can't go wrong.

> "'A Christmas Carol' is my favorite of all Dickens's short stories," said the professor.

Sometimes, we like to try and play with the mind of our computer and see if it can keep up with the strength of our punctuation knowledge! One such example is when we need to put quotation marks within a quotation mark. It can send your computer a little bit haywire if you are not careful. When quoting the name of a short story, poem or article when also quoting what someone else has written, use only one quotation mark. As you can see in the above example, the name of the short story comes at the beginning of the sentence, which means you have three quotation marks in a row. It is strictly correct, however, if you can restructure the sentence to avoid this, it is much more pleasing to the eye and won't send your computer into a download spiral of grammar confusion!

The end is now in sight, you have almost earned your badge for being a punctuation pro. Let's wrap it up with parentheses. A very useful punctuation mark, mainly because of our love of embellishing our sentences with additional information, the parenthesis is used to denote additional information within a sentence.

While climbing the stairs (paying more attention to his phone than his feet), Juan tripped and fell.

The main test for using parentheses is does the sentence make sense without the additional information? If it does, then you have a good case to use parentheses. Make sure that you always use them in pairs to surround the additional information and add a punctuation mark such as a comma, colon, or period, directly after the last parenthesis. In this example, the additional information is not needed for the meaning to remain the same, that Juan tripped on the stairs. Yet, its addition adds useful insight into why he fell.

My assignment is to write about the North Atlantic Treaty Organization (NATO) with my classmate (Jessica).

This example is a test. Can you see which word is correctly put in parentheses and which one is not? Let me help you out. NATO has been placed correctly in parentheses because it is an acronym of the North Atlantic Treaty Organization. It is more commonly known by its acronym so its addition to the sentence adds clarity for the reader. You will notice that you don't include punctuation after an acronym in parentheses. I must warn you though that our use of acronyms has gotten wildly out of control. We use acronyms for everything, particularly in the corporate business world. Don't just stick in an acronym for every long name or concept, only use the ones that are widely known by the general public. I do know that when you are fighting for word space in your papers at college, you want to use an acronym to save on space and time. However, have mercy on your professor who just doesn't want to read that the FTA has commissioned the HRH to work on behalf of the NWRA in partnership with the SPRCAN. Stuffing sentences with acronyms is painful and to be avoided.

The mistake in the example is that Jessica, the name of the person's classmate, should not be in parentheses. Even though it is additional information and the sentence makes sense with or without its inclusion, you simply add a comma and then place the name.

Lastly, let's talk about square brackets. These super helpful guys are a form of parentheses that you can use to add clarity to quotes. You can insert words into quotes to make them easier to read.

> It was written in the monthly report that, "The
> desired effect [of the presentation] was achieved,
> everyone clapped and cheered."

As you can see in the example, square brackets have been used to ensure that the reader knows that what is being talked about is the presentation. It is a small addition to the quote to ensure the meaning is translated correctly. Keep in mind that when using square brackets, the additional information should be very brief and concise. One of the main purposes of square brackets is for quoting the work of other people. So, if you add information into their quote that manipulates the meaning to something it is not meant to be, you are headed for trouble.

And there you have it, folks! We have come to the end of our sojourn through essential English language punctuation. I am certain by now that you will have a much more thorough understanding of when and when not to use the different punctuation marks. You know what I am going to say, practice makes perfect, so go through the examples as much as you can. That way, you can proudly show off your pro skills, with newfound confidence born from finally knowing what a semicolon actually is.

RULE 5 – PERFECT PAST, PRESENT AND FUTURE TENSE

One thing you can guarantee in life is that the seconds turn into minutes, minutes to hours, hours to days, and days to years. Time keeps marching on, whether or not we like it. What that means for our use of English grammar is that we have to be able to capture the fact that some things are happening now, some things have already happened, and some things are going to happen. To be able to cope with our time organized existence, the English language is written in tenses: present, past, and future.

In short, the present tense expresses what is happening right now, or something which is ongoing. The past tense expresses something that has already happened. The future tense expresses what might happen in the future. It sounds simple enough, doesn't it?

Well, the truth is, as is with lots of English grammar, there are a couple of different ways to use each tense correctly. What is more, a very common trait when writing in English is for writers to switch between tenses incorrectly. The reason is that, as with lots of English, you can use the tenses in exceptional ways whereby you may use a past tense verb to actually talk about the present. We do this an awful lot when speaking and the result is that we have transferred this trait to our written word. The best advice is to keep it simple and stick to the rules. There is never a justified reason to create overly complicated grammatical structures. Learn now which tense is which and focus on sticking to the right tense for the situation you are writing about.

Live in the present: understanding the present tense

With all the tenses we will go through, there is a simple version, a not so simple version, and a slightly more not so simple version. I wish it was all just one easy to understand concept but unfortunately, it is not. Not to fear, I am going to break down each variety so you can see how to use it correctly.

Simple present

I **am** happy to learn grammar, as I **write** every day.

This is an example of the simple present tense. It is used to describe what you are doing right now, such as right now I **am** happy to learn grammar. It is also used to describe a habitual activity that you do regularly. In this case, I **write** every day. The simple present tense is not difficult to conjugate as the majority of verbs for all pronouns use the root form of the verb, or add s or es to it.

First-person singular	I write
Second-person singular	You write
Third-person singular	He/She/It writes
First-person plural	We write
Second-person plural	You write
Third-person plural	They write

The notable exception to the simple conjugation of the simple present tense is the verb to be. It doesn't follow the above rule and just needs to be learned.

First-person singular	I am
Second-person singular	You are
Third-person singular	He/She/It is
First-person plural	We are
Second-person plural	You are
Third-person plural	They are

I **do not** want to go to the park.

To make a simple present tense verb negative, you can add the words do not (or shorten it to don't), before the verb.

I am **not** happy.

For the verb to be, you add **not** after the verb to make it negative.

I **have traveled** to China before.

Present perfect

The present perfect tense is the next version of the present tense and one which can trip people. The reason is that it is used to describe something that has happened in the past but without giving a definite time period or it can be used to show something that started in the past and continues to the present. In this example, the word **have** is added before a past tense verb to show that this person has traveled to China but it is not known when they did.

The present perfect tense is easy to conjugate by adding either have or has before a past tense verb.

First-person singular	I have traveled
Second-person singular	You have traveled
Third-person singular	He/She/It has traveled
First-person plural	We have traveled

Second-person plural	You have traveled
Third-person plural	They have traveled

To make a present perfect tense verb negative, you can add the words **not** after the word **have or has**.

I have **not** traveled to China before.

Present continuous

The present continuous tense is the final version of the present tense which we will talk about. It is used to describe a situation happening right now or in the very near future.

The taxi **is waiting** outside for you.

In this example, you can see that the action is happening right at that moment and is continuing to happen. It is a really useful way to conjugate a verb in the present tense. The verb is **waiting** and it is made continuous by adding the word **is** before it.

The present continuous tense is easy to conjugate by adding the verb to be to the present participle (meaning it has **ing** at the end of the verb).

First-person singular	I am waiting
Second-person singular	You are waiting
Third-person singular	He/She/It is waiting
First-person plural	We are waiting
Second-person plural	You are waiting
Third-person plural	They are waiting

To make a present continuous tense verb negative, you can add the words **not** after the verb to be.

I am **not** waiting any longer.

Looking to the past: understanding the past tense

As you can see by its name, the past tense is all about actions that took place already. Even though this seems easy to navigate, it can be tricky as we commonly misuse the past tense by mixing it up with the present tense in sentences. Just check through your work, paying close attention to your tenses, to ensure you have conjugated the verbs consistently in the same tense.

Simple past

I **learned** a lot from my English professor.

This is an example of the simple past tense. It simply describes an action that takes place in the past.

The simple past tense is not difficult to conjugate as long as the verb is regular. You mainly add ed to the end of the root verb.

First-person singular	I learned
Second-person singular	You learned
Third-person singular	He/She/It learned
First-person plural	We learned
Second-person plural	You learned

Third-person plural	They learned

When it comes to irregular verbs, however, it is a bit rockier. Below is a common example, but for most you must learn them by heart.

First-person singular	I was
Second-person singular	You were
Third-person singular	He/She/It was
First-person plural	We were
Second-person plural	You were
Third-person plural	They were

That is strange, I **did not** learn anything from that professor.

When it comes to making a simple past verb negative, it is not quite as simple. You must add the words **did not** before a root verb. This can trip you up as it looks like a present tense sentence.

I **was not** happy.

For the verb to be, you add **was not or were not** after the verb to make it negative.

Past perfect

I was shocked to discover that my dog **had eaten** the entire birthday cake.

The past perfect tense is an interesting tense used to describe a sequence of events that took place in the past. It is not used as commonly as the simple past tense, which does lead to common misunderstandings on how to use it. If you remember it as a way to recount actions that have taken place in a certain order in the past, you will find no problem with it.

In the above example, the simple past tense is first used to explain that the person was shocked. Why was the person shocked? It is because the dog **had eaten** the entire birthday cake. The **had eaten** is written in past perfect tense and is part of a sequence of events. First the person expressed they were shocked and then they said why.

Luckily, the past perfect tense is simpler to conjugate than to understand. To conjugate it you only have to add **had** before a past participle.

First-person singular	I had eaten
Second-person singular	You had eaten
Third-person singular	He/She/It had eaten
First-person plural	We had eaten
Second-person plural	You had eaten
Third-person plural	They had eaten

To make a past perfect tense verb negative, you add the words **not** after the word **had**.

They demanded I leave the restaurant even though I **had not** eaten yet.

Past continuous

The past continuous tense is the final version of the past tense which I will mention. It is used to describe a situation that happened in the past over a period of time.

Even though the sun **was shining** all summer, I could not find happiness in it.

In this example, you can see that the action of the sun shining happened in the past over a period of time which is defined as the summer. As I have mentioned before, this is one tense that people mix with the present tense when writing, so keep in mind the purpose of it.

The past continuous tense is conjugated by adding **was** or **were** to the present participle (meaning it has **ing** at the end of the verb).

First-person singular	I was waiting
Second-person singular	You were waiting
Third-person singular	He/She/It was waiting
First-person plural	We were waiting

Second-person plural	You were waiting
Third-person plural	They were waiting

To make a past continuous tense verb negative, you can add the words **not** after the verb to be.

Don't worry, I was **not** waiting for too long.

Dreaming of the future: understanding the future tense

Finally, we will take a look at the future tense. Arguably it's the most exciting tense, as who doesn't like dreaming of future plans. This tense is all about things that have not happened yet but that we want to talk about anyway. This might be so you can make future plans with your friends or predict the score of the footie game.

Simple future

By the end of the year, I **will learn** a new language.

This is an example of the simple future tense that talks of learning a new language in the future.

The simple future tense is not difficult to conjugate as you either add **will** before a root verb or you add **am/is/are going to** plus the root verb.

First-person singular	I will learn
Second-person singular	You will learn
Third-person singular	He/She/It will learn
First-person plural	We will learn
Second-person plural	You will learn
Third-person plural	They will learn

Even though it is easy to conjugate, the simple future can be confusing as you can have two ways to say the same thing.

| First-person singular | I am going to learn |
| Second-person singular | You are going to learn |

Third-person singular	He/She/It is going to learn
First-person plural	We are going to learn
Second-person plural	You are going to learn
Third-person plural	They are going to learn

As you can see, I will learn and I am going to learn are both in the simple future tense and both mean the same thing. The difference is that using **will** is considered formal and using **going to** is considered informal.

You **will not** learn anything if you don't stop talking over the class.

To make a simple future tense negative that uses **will,** simply add **not** after it.

This year will be not be any different, I am **not going to** learn French no matter what I promised myself on New Years' Eve.

To make a simple future tense negative that uses **going to,** add **not** before it.

Future perfect

By the time I arrive, **he will have** left.

The future perfect tense may look like it has been designed to catch you out but it isn't as nonsensical as it appears. Okay, yes you do use a past tense verb to describe something that has not happened yet. However, when you think about it, there is no other way to describe it. As you can see in this example, the future perfect tense is for describing something happening in the future that is dependent upon something else happening first. By the time the person arrives, which is the first part in a sequence of events, the other person **will have left.** The latter part is the future perfect tense.

The good news is that the future perfect tense is easy to conjugate. Add **will have** to a past tense verb to show that this has yet to happen.

First-person singular	I will have left
Second-person singular	You will have left
Third-person singular	He/She/It will have left

First-person plural	We will have left
Second-person plural	You will have left
Third-person plural	They will have left

To make a future perfect tense verb negative, you add the words **not** before the word **have**.

If you are lucky, they will **not** have left yet.

Future continuous

The future continuous tense is the final version of the future tense which we will cover. Its function is to describe something that will happen in the future over a period of time.

I am very proud to announce that my sister **will be running** the marathon this year.

In this example, you can see that her sister **will be running** the marathon. It is a great way to conjugate in the future as it emphasises the continuous nature of the action that will take place over a period of time. Something to note, you can only use the future continuous for action verbs such as running, walking, swimming, etc. If you try and conjugate it using a verb that doesn't describe an active action, it will appear ironic and odd to the reader. Just stick to the simple future tense for those verbs.

The future continuous tense is conjugated by adding **will be** to a present participle verb (meaning it has **ing** at the end of the verb).

First-person singular	I will be running
Second-person singular	You will be running
Third-person singular	He/She/It will be running
First-person plural	We will be running
Second-person plural	You will be running
Third-person plural	They will be running

To make a future continuous tense verb negative, you can add the word **not** in between will and be.

Due to an injury, Jessica will **not** be running today.

That is everything you are going to get from me in terms of tenses. There are a few extra tenses that you can use. However, my advice is that the tenses described above are by far the most commonly used and have you covered for whichever situation you wish to describe. Approach cautiously when starting to use tenses. Question your old habits as much as you can and ask yourself if you have broken away from mixing up the tenses. Don't worry, run through the examples a few more times to get more familiar and you will be just fine!

RULE 6 – STRUCTURING SENTENCES WITH EASE

We have learned about a wide variety of different grammar rules including, different tenses, punctuation and the basic building blocks. Yet, these rules don't mean anything by themselves. To actually write, we have to take everything that we have learned so far and put it into a sentence. This is what we are going to achieve in this chapter. It is not a difficult task by any means. What we must keep in mind is the basics of the rules we have learned so far and use them in an uncomplicated manner to form simple but effective sentences. I will cover a range of different sentence structures. By the end of this chapter you will have strong repertoire of writing structures that you can roll in any situation.

I could never have imagined that when I turned thirty I would have the opportunity to become the one thing I had always wanted to be. This was something I had dreamed about for a long time, finally it was here, finally I was a mother.

I wanted to show you this example to demonstrate what I mean by overly complicated sentence structure. It takes a long time to get to the point that the writer is trying to make. It is also contains a lot of redundant information that adds very little to the meaning of the two sentences.

When I turned thirty I fulfilled a lifelong dream of becoming a mother.

When we rewrite the information to form a concise and well formed sentence, we get the impact of the meaning immediately, with all redundant information removed. Many people feel that they want to pack their sentences with as much emotion as possible, yet this often leads to long and confusing sentences. Don't underestimate the power of a small well-formed sentence. Always aim to write in this way.

Before we get to sentences, we must look to phrases and clauses first. This is going to be a quick overview as I don't want to weigh you down with the technical side of sentence structure. You must be aware of the following but the structuring of sentences is much more important, especially knowing how to keep them concise and meaningful.

Phrases

A phrase is a group of related words that function together to represent something. There are different types of phrases which you can identify by what type of building block word they are using.

Noun phrase	Verb phrase	Adjective phrase	Adverb phrase	Prepositional phrase
the tiny baby	was playing	very small	truly beautiful	beside the bed

Phrases as you can see are collections of words. What is important to remember is that they can't be a complete sentence by themselves. Clauses on the other hand, though they look a lot like phrases, can stand alone more times than not and that is because they contain a verb.

Clauses

There are two main types of clauses, independent and dependent.

The art of Shiatsu massage was unknown in the Western World.

In this example, you can see an independent clause. If we analyze the sentence, there are several phrases within it. **The art of Shiatsu massage** is a noun phrase and **was unknown** is a verb phrase. We can identify it as an independent clause as it has a verb and the sentence is complete and understandable.

An independent clause is made up of a subject and a verb, also called a predicate. It stands alone as a sentence as it expresses a complete thought. When examining a sentence, if it is a simple case of a subject plus a verb with a period at the end, then this an independent clause.

Until Jessica returned

In contrast, this example represents a dependent clause. It is clear it is not a full sentence as it does not have any punctuation mark at the end. What is more, even if it did have a period at the end, it can't be complete. That is because the adverb **until** needs to be completed, you must ask yourself until what? On top of this, you must not confuse a dependent clause with a phrase. This is not a verb phrase as it contains more than just a noun and a verb, it also has an adverb in it.

Until Jessica returned, her dog would sit looking out of the window waiting for her.

Dependent clauses provide additional information to independent clauses as they can't stand alone by themselves.

In this example, you can see that the dependent clause has been added to an independent clause to show what was happening until Jessica returned.

Sentences

Now we get to the good stuff, sentences. We are going to go through the four main types of sentence structure which are simple sentences, compound sentences, complex sentences, and compound-complex sentences.

Simple Sentences

A simple sentence has one independent clause with one subject and one verb. As well as the subject and verb, a simple sentence can also have adjectives and adverbs. What a simple sentence can't have is another independent clause or dependent clause within it.

Jessica returned from work at six each day.

In this example, you can see that there is one subject, **Jessica**, and one verb, **returned**. Nothing has been added to the sentence other than nouns and adverbs. This is the trick to check whether it is a simple sentence or not.

Juan married within a year.

One subject and one verb can be seen again in this example. It is a powerful example as it demonstrates how to deliver a sentence concisely and with oomph! Simple sentences are a great tool to have in your bag. They can be used to deliver poignant messages. You often see them used in literature and other creative writing. That is because a good author knows that you don't need to fluff out your sentences to deliver the message effectively.

Compound sentences

As much as I am a fan of short, concise sentences, I'll admit that there is a need to say a little bit more sometimes. Enter center stage the compound sentence. A compound sentence combines two or more independent clauses to make a complete sentence. The independent clauses are connected with a conjunction such as for, and, but, or, etc. If you are really brave, you could also use a semicolon to connect them together.

We traveled all day to get here and now you want me to leave?

Remember that a compound sentence contains two or more independent clauses. In this example it is clear that there are two separate parts. First we talk about travelling all day. This clause is independent as it has a subject and a verb. Second we talk about being told to leave. This clause is also independent because it too has a subject and a verb. You could, in theory, place a period after the first clause and not use a conjunction. However, the reason a conjunction is used and a compound sentence is necessary is that these two bits of information directly relate to each other. The use of a compound sentence emphasizes that despite traveling all day they are being told to leave. How rude!

Complex sentences

Don't worry, these aren't actually complicated. A complex sentence joins one independent clause with at least one dependent clause. The independent clause is called the main clause and is linked to the dependent clause with a subordinating conjunction. This type of conjunction includes the adverbs until, while, and even though.

Jessica's dog would not rest until she returned.

This example shows you that complex sentences don't have to be long. The first part of the sentence about Jessica's dog represents the main clause as it is an independent clause. We can tell this because it has a subject, **Jessica's dog**, and it has a verb, **would not rest**. We also know it is an independent clause because it could be a complete sentence by itself. To make this a complex sentence, a dependent clause has been attached using a subordinating conjunction. This is the **until**

she returned part. Despite having a subject and a verb in this clause, as it has **until** at the start of the sentence, it can't stand alone as a complete sentence.

While I cooked dinner, Jessica took the dog out for a walk.

Complex sentences can also start with the dependent clause that is joined to the main clause by a comma. Remember though that the dependent clause must start with a subordinating conjunction. This structure works well with **while** and **even though**.

Compound-Complex Sentences

Finally, we come to our fourth type of sentence structure, the ultimate compound-complex sentence structure. A compound-complex sentence has at least two independent clauses and at least one dependent clause. Yes, it may sound like a recipe for a long and convoluted sentence, and it is. Pay attention when using this structure to adding in unnecessary information. Keep it neat and concise. If you do this, you can impress with this type of structure. Fail at it and your page turns into a mess of confusion. No pressure then!

I planned to go to the mall, but I couldn't until the postman delivered the post.

Let's break up the sentence to see the different parts. The first part, **I planned to go to the mall,** is an independent clause. It has a subject and a verb. It can also be a complete sentence. The second part, **but I couldn't until,** is a dependent clause that uses a subordinating conjunction. The third part, **the postman delivered the post,** is also an independent clause. It too has a subject and a verb. It could be a complete sentence by itself but importantly it would have a different meaning if it did stand alone. All together, the sum of these parts qualifies this sentence to be a compound-complex sentence.

You now know the four different types of sentences and you should be confident in using them correctly. Whenever you are faced with deciding which type of sentence structure to use, keep in mind that it should be short and to the point.

There are a few additional bits of advice I can offer you to keep you from forming sloppy sentences. Firstly, never join the two independent clauses in a compound sentence with a comma, potentially also adding a third or fourth independent clause this way. This I call comma splicing and it results in a long sentence with unrelated information grouped together.

Secondly, your choice of sentence structure should depend upon who you are talking to. If your audience is children then using compound-complex sentences is inappropriate. Likewise, when trying to impress your boss, relying only on simple sentences can make your writing appear childlike. There is a fine balance to strike.

Lastly, as you develop your style, you will come to favor certain sentence structures. This is a good thing as it designates your writing as yours. Often, the sentence structures you come to use mirror the way you speak. Be mindful of this and be careful not to waffle. However, if complex sentences become your go-to sentence structure, then that is just fine. Keep them concise and full of rhythm. That way your writing style will be well pronounced on the page.

Now you have learned your sentence structures and can tell your way around an independent clause or dependent clause, it is time to practice. Go through each type of sentence structure and write out 4 or 5 examples of your own. Once you have done this, leave them for a while and return to check them later. When you check them, did you only put related information into each sentence? Did you correctly form a compound sentence rather than mixing it with a complex sentence? Be critical of what you have written. You are looking for bad habits that you may have developed. I am trying to break you of those habits so you can go forward from now only using correct sentence structure.

RULE 7 – CONQUER CAPITALIZATION

It is fair to say, we have a problem with capitalization. This problem has developed so much that we now frantically place capital letters on everything. My advice, calm down. We are going to clear up this mess once and for all. By the end of this chapter you will be confidently placing capital letters only where needed. Let's go through them one by one.

The first word of a sentence begins with a capital letter.

My mother is coming to visit us. **W**e need to clean the entire house. **N**ow!

The names of the days of the week, and of the months of the year, are written with a capital letter.

Next **F**riday, **T**uesday, 21 **J**anuary, there will be no classes.

The names of historical eras are capitalized.

Today, we will study the **I**ron **A**ge.

The names of holy festivals and holidays should be capitalized.

The children were so excited they stayed awake until **C**hristmas morning.

The names of languages are written with a capital letter.

I am studying **E**nglish literature, geography, and math.

Words that are related to a particular place must be written with a capital letter.

I am meeting with the French ambassador.

However, if a word related to a particular place is part of a phrase, you do not capitalize it.

I could eat a danish pastry every morning, but I shouldn't.

Proper nouns should have a capital letter. Be careful not to capitalize words that look like they could be a proper noun but are in fact just a common noun. Normally, these are the names of professions, such as doctor, president, manager, etc.

Jessica is our new student body president.

You will find that religious names and terms are often capitalized. These may be names of different religions, gods, important figures, and holy books.

The **Q**uran is a holy book for **M**uslims.

The name of a book, play, poem, film, magazine, newspaper or piece of music should be capitalized. Remember that whenever you have a conjunction or article in the title, these should not be capitalized.

Harry **P**otter and the **S**orcerer's **S**tone is the favorite book of many children.

The brand names of manufacturers and any of their products are always capitalized.

Ever since I was a young man, my dream has been to buy a **F**errari.

When quoting someone directly, the first letter in the quote should be capitalized only when what is quoted is a complete sentence. Luckily, this is most of the time.

The French philosopher Descartes is the author of "**I** think, therefore I am."

Keep in mind, some brand names have become so popular that they are now used to describe the entire product category. In this case they are no longer capitalized.

I would like to buy some scotch tape.

The pronoun I is always capitalized but other pronouns are not.

I am going into the city today.

A notable exception to this is when talking about God in various religions. In this case, the pronoun he/him is capitalized. This is to show respect.

It is by the grace of God that **He** will decide whether or not I will be forgiven.

When writing a title there are two different ways to capitalize. The first style is to capitalize all principle words. What this means is anything that is not a conjunction or an article.

The **E**ssential **G**uide to **L**earning **F**rench

The second style is to only capitalize the first letter of the title. This is called sentence style. It does not matter which you choose, what is important is that you are consistent.

The essential guide to learning French

It is now important to talk about examples where capitalization is often used incorrectly. The mistake usually occurs when people feel that a word should be emphasized.

Smoking is STRICTLY forbidden.

Instead of capitalizing the word, if you want to stress the word use italics.

Capitalizing a word because it is proceeded by **the** is also a common mistake. It may appear that the word is a proper noun because there is an article before it, however, only proper nouns should be capitalized.

He was the first person to reach the South Pole.

This example is incorrect. Rather, it should be the south pole.

When writing about a concept this should not be capitalized.

I was inspired by Psychoanalysis and the work of Sigmund Freud.

The correct version is to not capitalize psychoanalysis.

Finally, don't capitalize everything just because it is a name. We have spoken about our love of names, so there are a lot of them. When you want to talk about a name, focus on the correct rule. If it is a proper noun, use a capital letter. If it is commonly used then don't use a capital letter.

I went to see the Doctor today but I couldn't see my Doctor. Instead they sent me to see Doctor Singh.

In this example, only one use of the word doctor is correctly capitalized. The version that should have a capital letter is Doctor Singh as it is a title of a person.

Overall, there are quite a few different rules for capitalization. The thing to keep in mind is that you likely have a bad habit of excessive capitalization. We panic when we write and stick a capital letter on everything. Take control of this bad habit and instead focus on what it is you are talking about. On the whole, if it is a specific thing you capitalize it. If it is a general thing, you don't capitalize it.

RULE 8 – SPELL CORRECTLY AND FORMAT EFFICIENTLY

Spelling correctly terrifies most adults. We are held captive by our spell checkers to ensure we don't embarrass ourselves with our poor spelling. Often, we are scarred by years of English teachers telling us our spelling is terrible. This has to stop. Once and for all, we as functioning adults need to take control of our bad spelling and learn how to spell.

Learned bad behavior is a difficult habit to break. When you write anything, I am certain that you make the same five to ten spelling errors each time. I know this is true, because we all do it. That is because when you first learned English as a child you will have incorrectly memorized spellings of commonly misspelled words. Rather than correcting the mistake then, this error has haunted your writing ever since. For me, it is the word separate. Every time I am typing quickly on the laptop,

I write it as seperate. When I make this error, the red line of my spell checker shows up and I right click it to correct the spelling. This is an incredibly bad habit as I don't always have my trusty spell checker on hand.

Spelling common words incorrectly is glaringly obvious when people read through your work. That is why relearning spelling as an adult is vital. Don't let the quality of your work be jeopardized by poor spelling. Instead, let us now both embark on breaking our bad habits and start to relearn how to spell correctly.

Let us go through the five top rules for spelling better, starting with I before E except after C unless it sounds like an A.

A **pie**ce of cake

In this example, I goes before E because the letter before it is a P.

He dec**ei**ved me.

But when the letter before it is a C, you switch the letters.

How much do you w**ei**gh?

As well, if the combination of E and I sounds like an A, you also write it ei and not ie.

The next spelling tip is about adding suffixes. You tend to do this when you are trying to make a word a superlative or comparative.

He was the ugli**est** baby I had ever seen.

The mistake people make is trying to add er to words that end in Y. They might try and say uglyer rather than uglier. The rule to remember is that if the word ends in Y it is most likely irregular in the way you conjugate the superlative or comparative. Most of the time you remove the Y and add something there to make the suffix correct.

I will happ**ily** attend your party.

The same rule applies for words ending in y when you are trying to form an adverb. Always replace the Y with an I and add the standard ly ending.

When to add an E or not is also something that often confuses us. This is because the E when coming at the end of a word is often not pronounced.

"I **bit** off more than I can chew with this one," said Jessica.

"No, not at all. Her bark is worse than her **bite**, trust me," said Juan.

The words bit and bite are commonly misspelled even though when you pronounce them they do sound different. On the whole remember verbs tend to not end in E and nouns do. This should help you to remember which is the correct spelling for each case.

Words containing double consonants, sometimes two or more sets of them, are difficult to spell correctly. That is because when we sound them out it is difficult to distinguish whether there is one consonant sound or two.

I am looking for some a**ccomm**odation.

To overcome these spelling errors, slow down and sound out the word beat by beat. Ac-com-mo-dation. As you can see, by doing this, we can identify that there are double consonants being used.

Our last spelling rule is knowing how to make a word plural. We often trip up over whether to put an s or es on the end or even not add anything. The rule goes that if the word ends in either -*s*, -*sh*, -*ch*, -*x*, or -*z*, then you add -*es*.

In the morning I only have to take two train**s** but my sister has to take three bus**es**.

There is also the classic example of how many sheep are in the field?

Farmer John has one **sheep** but Farmer Tom has three **sheep**.

With the common words sheep and fish, there is no difference between the singular and plural form. There are just sheep and never sheeps.

I appreciate that going through the rules of spelling probably feels like you are back in the classroom again. I am certain that you know the I before E except after C rule. Yet, I am also certain you commonly misspell words with ie in them. So, what do we do about this? It is time to put effort behind breaking this habit.

Firstly, try to read more. Grab an article each day and sit for ten minutes to read it. This will expose your eyes to correct spelling for a variety of words that you are probably misspelling.

Next, write a list of the words you commonly misspell. Every time a word is highlighted by your spell checker as incorrect, jot it down somewhere. If you are active in alerting your brain to the mistake, next time you come to spell it you will pause for a moment and think about the correct spelling.

Lastly, try and go through the rules above and memorise the rules through a little poem or rhyme. I before E except after C is memorable because it rhymes. This is called a mnemonic. Try and make more for other spelling errors you make. This type of memory technique is easily memorable as it breaks through walls you put up about certain issues and brings the correct information to the front of your mind.

Spelling incorrectly is one very noticeable trait. The other is not formatting your work in a consistent way. Having different font sizes, excessive amounts of space and incorrect paragraph spacing can make your work look amateurish. As with spelling, don't let a poorly formatted document keep you from making the best impression. Let's run through the top tips for formatting efficiently.

The first tip is to insert only one space after a period and not two. The idea of placing two spaces after a period comes from the need of typesetters with printing presses to clearly identify each sentence. With modern word processors, this is no longer necessary. What is more it can mess up your formatting, particular the margin indent when you justify your text if you continue this old fashioned method.

The second tip is to know how to get an em-Dash to appear on your page without sending your computer into a spin. Just hit alt/option + shift + dash (-) at the same time and you'll get the long em-dash. If you want an en-Dash rather than em-Dash, use the shortcut alt/option + dash (-).

The third tip is for using an ellipse, which is when you want to end your sentences dramatically with . . . If you simply add in three periods, with or without spacing, it can confuse the formatting machine in your word processor. Make sure it is understood as an ellipse by using the shortcut alt/option + semicolon (;).

The fourth tip is for spelling out numbers. There is a difference in opinion of how to write numbers in your work. In all correctness, you should write out numbers from one to ninety-nine, placing a hyphen between any that are two words. However, it has become acceptable to only spell out numbers one through nine and then use numerals for the rest of the numbers.

At **one** in the morning, the temperature was minus **17** degrees.

The fifth tip is when you talk about a percentage that you write the word out in full rather than using the symbol.

There is a 20 **percent** discount.

The sixth tip is to use only three sizes of fonts throughout your document. The header should be around 18 pts, subheaders should be around 14 pts and the body text should be around 12 pts. Make sure that the font you use is the same throughout the document. The same goes for the color of the text.

The last tip is to keep your paragraphs short. The best size to stick to is around five to six lines. This makes it much easier for a reader to read as well as keeping their attention for longer. When a paragraph is too long, readers have a tendency to skip to the end of the paragraph as they assume that is where the important information is.

In sum, spelling and formatting may seem like the icing on the cake. However, they can make or break your work. I know personally that some people will not hire someone who has a spelling error in their resume. Don't let something that is easily correctable stand in the way of getting your dream job or opportunity. Learn the advice given in this chapter and you will quickly mark yourself out against your competitors as someone with excellent writing skills.

RULE 9 – CREATE KILLER COMPOSITIONS

You have almost made it, you have made it through the essential building blocks of the English language, how to use punctuation and write different sentence structures. Now is the time to use everything you have learned and write.

In whichever situation you find yourself in, whether you are working in an office or a student at college, you will have to write long essays or reports. These essays will typically be over 500 words. Even though you understand how to form perfect sentences, you now need to know how to form these into a well structured essay. This is where having killer composition skills is essential.

There is nothing worse than having to battle your way through long and unstructured written work. If someone is waffling, going off point, and not being concise, it makes the reading experience unpleasant. What is more, the reader can't focus on the important information and loses concentration.

All of these things are avoidable by learning how to structure your essay correctly. So first let's talk about different types of essays and then move on to creating a killer composition that will never bore your readers.

There are four types of essays that you can write. Firstly, there is a narrative essay. This is when the writer describes an incident or story written in the first person. You might do this when reporting upon your own findings or when writing a creative piece. The aim when writing narrative essays is to make the reader feel that they are right there with you in the story. Make the essay as dynamic as possible.

The next essay type is a descriptive essay. This is where the writer describes something usually from memory. The aim is to paint a picture with your words. One clever way to do that is to evoke the senses of the reader by talking about what you can see, smell, touch, hear, etc. You must appeal to the emotions of the reader and get them to empathize with what you are writing.

An expository essay presents a balanced study of a topic and is most commonly used when writing college essays. The essay should be well researched and show a balanced argument of the topic. The writing is not emotional and should be fact based. This includes using references to others work and things such as statistics, graphs, etc.

The last essay type is a persuasive essay. The purpose of this type of essay is to get the reader to see your side of the argument. It is most commonly used in work when you are asked to present a proposal of your ideas for the business. A persuasive essay is not just a presentation of facts but an attempt to convince the reader of the writer's point of view. The essay must present both sides of the argument but ultimately persuade the reader to agree with your side of the argument.

Once you know the type of essay that you want to write, it is then best to follow a few key rules for the layout of the essay. You can still be creative within these boundaries, but if you follow what is suggested you will avoid going off track. Focus on delivering the main message of the essay. Do not overcomplicate it with unnecessary information. Keep it concise and well formatted and you can't go wrong. Knock the socks off your college professor or boss by presenting them with your next essay written with a killer composition.

First off, all essays should start with an introduction. This is the first paragraph of your essay where you introduce your topic. It needs to include a brief overview of what you will write about. You can also include your main message in the introduction, this could be what you have found out. If you include this in your introduction it helps the reader focus throughout the rest of the paper as you explain how you came to this conclusion. This is called a hook message and works well when using all of the essays types that we went through. Just remember to keep everything short. You should not write an essay within an essay by spelling everything out in your introduction. On the whole, limit it to around five to six lines. Use impactful words to entice your reader to read on.

Then you must write the body of your essay. This is the main part of your essay. No matter the type of essay you are writing, the body should include more than one paragraph. Keep your paragraphs short. Move through your arguments logically, presenting them one by one and providing evidence for each of them. If you have separate topics that you want to mention, consider using subheadings to ensure that the reader understand what each section is. Build up the pressure within your essay, pulling your reader along with you, towards the peak of the overall argument that you are looking to make. Finish the body section with the main statement that you are looking to present.

Finally, always end all essays with a conclusion. Without it, it feels like a body without feet. Use your conclusion to sum up your story or argument. Make sure that you don't include any new information in your conclusion. Everything that you conclude must have been mentioned before. If you don't it can make your argument appear weak. Make sure to reiterate the overall message of the essay. Wrap up all the loose threads of the work and make sure to leave the reader with a punchy takeaway that will keep them thinking about your essay once they have put it down.

In sum, an essay is always something you find yourself being asked to write. It is important to make sure you are well practiced on the best way to structure your essay. The key thing is to ensure you deliver the message you want to make clearly. This doesn't mean you have to write pages after pages, going into excessive detail. Instead, keep it neat and tight. Write an introduction, body and conclusion that clearly demonstrates your argument.

RULE 10 – ADD YOUR PERSONAL TOUCH

Now that you are a writer it is time to develop your writing style. Also called your personal touch, your writing style is the way in which you express yourself and it naturally evolves over time. It changes as you age as you go through different stages of life, develop your own personality, change the activities you are involved in, and change what you are reading, along with many other factors. So, what can you do to develop your own writing style? Well, the truth is that a writing style depends upon life experience as well as the situation you are writing in. You may start off at college writing formally. Yet as you age, you become more informal in your style. What matters most is that you are consistent in your style. If you like to use emotive words, don't all of a sudden switch to being very clinical and cold.

There are many ways to develop your style and discover new ways to write. Read regularly and broadly. Aim to read a few full books a year. Articles are much quicker to read so skim through a few each week. Avoid anything that is not written in formal language. The aim here is to develop your writing style, not to pick up bad habits.

Don't avoid writing. I know that it might seem that presenting your great idea is quicker and more efficient. However, there is something incredibly powerful about a well written proposal. Take the time to write as much as you can. Also, focus on writing whatever you do write correctly. Don't allow yourself to continue bad habits just because it is a quick email or SMS. What about writing creatively as well? Not everything you write has to be for work or college. You might discover you have a talent for writing emotionally, something which suits poetry and short stories. This will help to develop your overall writing style and might make that next proposal a little less dry.

Use words that come naturally to you rather than trying to stuff your work with complicated terminology. Nobody likes a show-off, not to mention it risks the reader not being able to understand you. Instead focus on acquiring a variety of well known words. When you are writing, don't use the same word or phrase repeatedly. Try to learn synonyms for your regular words to broaden your vocabulary range.

Be as clear as you can. Remember that your main goal is communication. I have said it a million times but it does need repeating: make sure each sentence is as direct and simple as possible. At the same time, don't be overly clinical. If you are trying to convey emotions, you may need to pack your sentences with a few more adjectives and adverbs. Make your writing easy for your readers, so it is a pleasure to read. Awkward writing can make it painful and provoke your readers into putting down your work.

It is tough to do, but you really have to steer clear of clichés as much as possible. They can make your writing sound unoriginal. Sometimes you can use them for effect, especially if you are trying to evoke an emotion that only that cliché will deliver. Instead think of crafting your own descriptions, use metaphors and expressions. This will make what you write look original and stand out from the crowd.

When you are using different sentence structures, make sure that you are concise. Change the word order in your sentences to see if they can be rephrased using fewer words. Focus on being as concise as possible. At all costs, avoid long sentences with unrelated information contained within them. Don't comma-splice your way to drab, unreadable work.

Clear, detailed writing makes your work come to life. If you are struggling to find the right words for your descriptions, do a little research. It is easy to access a thesaurus online. The English language has over 250,000 words, so you have no excuse for not being able to find the perfect word for the situation you are trying to describe.

Finally, develop your style by using certain literary devices that come to define your work. If you like using metaphors or similes, this will provide a certain style to your writing. If you prefer technical writing, this will also define how you write.

> In this essay, I will demonstrate exactly why copper is an excellent insulator. To arrive at this conclusion, I undertook extensive research. My main research was conducted in the laboratory. I wanted to test my hypothesis that copper can be used in wires as an insulator. What is more, I wanted to prove that copper is the most suitable choice for this purpose over other metals. Overall, my hypothesis was proven correct.

As an example of a writing style, this represents a concise and well written introduction for a technical essay. It is clear that the writer prefers short clear sentences that deliver the meaning quickly.

It is clear to me that the best course of action is to abandon this job contract. Though it distresses me to say so, we will not gain anything further from this partnership. I am truly grateful for the hard work of all our colleagues. Their dedication shines through in everything they undertake.

This second example demonstrates that you can use more emotional language even when writing a professional piece of work. The message being delivered is clear but what is stronger still is the emotion of disappointment. This style of writing is an excellent way to convey emotion.

We are excited to announce the launch of our new product. Built by a team of world class engineers, this product will revolutionize the way that you wash your clothes. You no longer have to deal with holes in your favorite jumper or rips in your faded jeans. Get in touch with us today to find out how to get yours!

In this final example, you can see a mix of formal sentence structures with a more informal tone. This writing style is an excellent method for selling products. It demonstrates how you can write engaging content without having to compromise on your grammatical structures.

Overall, the thing about writing styles is that it is down to you. The best writing styles are developed naturally and reflect your personality. Keep in mind that just because something should be written formally, it doesn't mean it has to be bland. Write clearly but add flavor to what you write by using a mix of words and devices such as metaphors. Over time you will become comfortable with your style, being able to easily adapt it based on the situation.

BONUS RULE – NEVER NEGLECT COMMON GRAMMAR MISTAKES

Congratulations, you have made it through all of the steps in becoming an English grammar pro! We have covered everything from nouns and verbs to semicolons and the perfect future tense. By now you will have a thorough understanding of how to create incredible and accurate written work.

As you have been successful in completing all of the rules, here is a bonus rule to seal the deal! I am going to run through the top ten grammar mistakes so that you can learn to avoid discrediting your work by making one of them.

Finally, I have come to the conclusion, that I am ready, to take on the role of head teacher.

The number one mistake of all time is the misuse of commas. It is so rampant that we have come to see it as normal to have huge amounts of commas in a sentence. I am sure you have paused once or twice when writing to debate whether or not you should be using a comma. The problem is that people associate commas with a pause in speaking. This then translates to the page and ends up in a comma misuse. You can see in the above example that the person is clearly trying to emphasize the importance of the decision to become a teacher. However, by using commas in this way they have split clauses apart and rendered the sentence incorrect. The best advice is to lower your use of commas, not increase it.

At the mall I am going to buy: socks; shoes; makeup; and a bag.

Next to the comma, the semicolon is the most abused punctuation mark. As you can see in the above example, it is often used incorrectly and unnecessarily. The word unnecessary is the right word as the truth is the semicolon is largely unnecessary. What is more, it can make your writing appear pompous. I know it is a legitimate punctuation mark and people are desperate to not have it disappear into obscurity. However, if you have just recovered from being a grammar offender, steer clear of it and use a comma instead.

Rugby, which was first played in England in the early 18th century, is one of Australia's most popular sports.

This example may look harmless. However, the problem comes with two sets of unrelated information being contained in one sentence. What is trying to be achieved is a concept called parallelism. This concept aims to show information about a topic at the same time as delivering a different message about the same topic. It is meant to enhance your knowledge of the topic. However, what happens often is that the sentence structure gets confused. It is acceptable to have two sentences next to each other talking about rugby. Yet, combining them is incorrect. You might think it is fine because they are both about rugby, however they are not actually related as one sentence should be just about it being first played in England and the other about it being Australia's most popular sport. Remember the number one tip of this book, keep it simple, keep it short.

The business was founded by Ewan Evans.

This sentence is something that you will commonly see and it is written in what is called the passive voice. This example is not strictly a grammar mistake. Instead it is a writing style suggestion that you avoid using the passive voice wherever. It used to be considered a formal way of writing. The truth is that it leads to drab sentences that lack energy. Change the passive voice to the active voice by switching the word order to Ewan Evans founded the business. This way of writing is just as formal but more dynamic.

I was waiting their for over an hour.

Don't fall into the trap laid out for you by homophones. We went through them in detail in rule 3 so you should be well versed in how to recognize them. You know you will only incite ridicule if you make a silly mistake like using their instead of there.

The content was good.

If you were worried about homophones, wait till you see what homographs have in store for you! These words are spelled the same but have a different meaning. For example, the content was good has two different meanings. It could mean that a piece of content was good. In this case, the accent would go on the first beat. Rather, the sentence could refer to a feeling of satisfaction. In this case, the accent would go on the second beat. You have to be certain that the context of your sentence is clear if you are using a homograph. If not, change the word.

He went rapidly to the store.

Adverbs are not your friend. I know it might seem like they are but trust me they are not. Writers have a tendency to use an adverb which results in the death of description. This sentence should instead say he went to the store in a rush. It is much more descriptive and also gives the sense of urgency needed. However, the adverb doesn't do this, it simply says he went to the store with speed. The meaning is not as significant. Next time you place an adverb in a sentence, see if you can switch it out with a better description.

It is easy to forget what all this hard work is for.

Stop! Don't do it! I know we end our sentences in speaking with prepositions but you can never do this in written work. Change the sentence around so that it reads what all this hard work is for is easy to forget. Better still, rewrite the sentence so it is not so awkward. If you don't you risk your work looking informal and poorly formed. Stick to formal writing as much as you can and don't repeat this grammar mistake.

This is why I don't go to nightclubs, I easily get tired.

In this example, the mistake lies in the use of **this**. What is wrong is that it is not clear what the **this** is referring to. This mistake is called a dangling modifier. It is a mistake that lots of people make. The reason is that we assume that the reader is following our train of thought. Whereas in truth, the reader can easily get lost in your words and forget previous information they have been told. Even though in this example, you can make a reasonable assumption that the reason they don't go to nightclubs is because they easily get tired, this meaning is not guaranteed. You might have before it the sentence, I hate music. Then the reader might wonder whether they are not going to nightclubs because they hate music or because they easily get tired? As you can see, the meaning is hazy. Clear this up for your reader by not using the modifier. Change the sentence to I don't go to nightclubs because I easily get tired.

You can either have chocolate, strawberry, or vanilla ice cream.

In our final grammar mistake you are faced with an incorrect use of a conjunction. It is commonly done, particular with **either**. The mistake is that three nouns have been described after using the word **either**. The correct way to use this conjunction is only ever with two nouns. It is talking about an either/or situation so will only ever contain two items. We have gone through the use of every conjunction in detail in rule 4. Don't be caught out making a simple error like this. Go through all of the examples again and learn what is the right way to use each conjunction.

So there you have it, the top ten grammar mistakes made by our fellow grammar offenders. However, as you have now made it to the end of the book, officially, you are no longer a grammar offender. Rise up, oh learned person who has made it through the book, and take up your hallowed position as an English grammar aficionado!

CONCLUSION

I have always wanted to write this book because I know that there are so many people out there that struggle with the basics of grammar. I also know that this really isn't their fault. Due to a lack of schooling on English grammar and the rise of informal language that has edged its way into our written work, we have all suffered as a result.

My goal was to create a book that was accessible to all who see themselves as grammar offenders. I can imagine that you have earned this title because of a public shaming about your persistent grammatical mistakes. It might have been because of a harmless group email you sent out saying that your all welcome. Or perhaps your boss has pulled you up on your poorly formatted work. Whatever way it came about, I know it upset you enough to do something about it. I bet you are glad you finally have done something about it.

Now that you have reached the end of the book, you have covered everything you need to know to survive in the world of English grammar. More than that, you now have to the tools to truly develop yourself as a writer. I have mentioned in the book that you really can't get away from having to do written work, well unless you are a farmer I guess. Even if you avoid writing reports in your job right now, in the future you will have to submit a resume and a cover letter. This requires a whole host of writing skills to complete. Doesn't it feel great that you now have them?

We started the book discussing the building blocks of the English language, covering the differences between verbs, nouns, adjectives, and adverbs. Next, we moved on to understanding how to connect these words together with conjunctions and prepositions. We then looked at the confusing world of words that look and sound the same, so that you don't mistakenly use one incorrectly. Onwards, we spent a good time on punctuation, arguably the most difficult part of grammar. We then looked at the differences between the present, past and future tense. Next, was structuring sentences. This was where it all started to come together. We took a moment to conquer capitalization once and for all before moving on to learning how to spell and format correctly. Then we worked on how to write killer compositions before ending up with working on how to develop your own writing style.

As we have taken this journey through English grammar, my aim has always been to show you how to keep things simple. By not over complicating grammar and the way you write, the result is beautifully written concise work. If you focus only on this, you will always produce clear and understandable sentences. Over time, if you also read more and practice your spelling, you will soon develop advanced writing skills. Once you are at that level, grammar mistakes will be kept to a minimum and you can then focus on developing your own writing style.

I made you a promise at the start of this book that you would no longer feel lost and confused with grammar. Instead you rise as a grammar phoenix, strong enough to tackle even the most complex of grammar situations. If you have read through all of the rules and practiced the examples, then you will have significantly improved your knowledge of English grammar. You can now stand tall as a person who knows what is what in the world of grammar and can easily roll out a perfect composition, or two.

I leave you with this one parting remark, the crux of this book: keep it simple to not mess it up. If there is anything you take from this book, that is it. Grammar might seem like an untamable beast but if you don't get yourself involved with its unnecessary complexity then you won't make silly mistakes.

Write simply, with passion, and you can't go wrong.

RESOURCES

8 Steps to Write a Good Composition (part 1). (n.d.). Retrieved December 13, 2019, from https://multimedia-english.com/blog/8-steps-to-write-a-good-composition-part-1-1

Andrews, R. (2018, December 12). 3 Ways to Add a Personal Touch to Your Writing. Retrieved December 13, 2019, from https://mythicscribes.com/writing-techniques/personal-writing/

Edudose. (n.d.). English Grammar Tense Rules. Retrieved December 13, 2019, from https://www.edudose.com/english/grammar-tense-rules/

Fenlearning. (2017, September 27). Ten Tips for Better Spelling. Retrieved December 13, 2019, from https://www.infoplease.com/arts-entertainment/writing-and-language/ten-tips-better-spelling

Grammarbook.com. (n.d.). Capitalization | Punctuation Rules. Retrieved December 13, 2019, from https://www.grammarbook.com/punctuation/capital.asp

Grammarly. (2019, May 7). Spelling Rules. Retrieved December 13, 2019, from https://www.grammarly.com/blog/spelling/

Limited, W. (2018, January 11). Basic English punctuation. Retrieved December 13, 2019, from https://www.wordy.com/writers-workshop/basic-english-punctuation/

Logic of English - Spelling Rules. (n.d.). Retrieved December 13, 2019, from https://www.logicofenglish.com/resources/spelling-rules

Lukyanchuk, M. (2019, May 16). Capitalization. Retrieved

December 13, 2019, from
https://www.grammarly.com/blog/capitalization-rules/

MBA Rendevous. (2019, September 16). Definition of Tenses with Example, Types of Tenses - Past,... Retrieved December 13, 2019, from https://www.mbarendezvous.com/tense/

Moore, C. (n.d.). Explanation of Homonyms, Homophones, Homographs and Heteronyms. Retrieved December 13, 2019, from http://www.magickeys.com/books/riddles/words.html

Nordquist, R. (2018, March 31). The Basic Parts and Structures of English Sentences. Retrieved December 13, 2019, from https://www.thoughtco.com/sentence-parts-and-sentence-structures-1689671

Synatex. (n.d.). Sentence Structure. Retrieved December 13, 2019, from https://www.syntaxis.com/sentence-structure

The Basics of Punctuation | SkillsYouNeed. (n.d.). Retrieved December 13, 2019, from https://www.skillsyouneed.com/write/punctuation1.html

University of North Carolina. (2019, July 1). Verb Tenses. Retrieved December 13, 2019, from https://writingcenter.unc.edu/tips-and-tools/verb-tenses/

Vocabulary.com. (n.d.). homonym vs. homophone vs. homograph on Vocabulary.com. Retrieved December 13, 2019, from https://www.vocabulary.com/articles/chooseyourwords/homonym-homophone-homograph/

Wordy. (2018, January 11). Basic English sentence structure. Retrieved December 13, 2019, from https://www.wordy.com/writers-workshop/basic-english-sentence-structure/

CPSIA information can be obtained
at www.ICGtesting.com
Printed in the USA
BVHW032141120421
604792BV00001B/25